Leaders in conflict

Manchester University Press

Leaders in conflict

Bush and Rumsfeld in Iraq

Stephen Benedict Dyson

Manchester University Press
Manchester and New York

distributed in the United States exclusively
by Palgrave Macmillan

Published by Manchester University Press
Oxford Road, Manchester M13 9NR, UK
and Room 400, 175 Fifth Avenue, New York, NY 10010, USA
www.manchesteruniversitypress.co.uk

Distributed in the United States exclusively by
Palgrave Macmillan, 175 Fifth Avenue, New York,
NY 10010, USA

Distributed in Canada exclusively by
UBC Press, University of British Columbia, 2029 West Mall,
Vancouver, BC, Canada V6T 1Z2

British Library Cataloguing-in-Publication Data
A catalogue record for this book is available from the British Library

Library of Congress Cataloging-in-Publication Data applied for

ISBN   978 0 7190 9170 4   hardback

First published 2014

The publisher has no responsibility for the persistence or accuracy of URLs for any external or third-party internet websites referred to in this book, and does not guarantee that any content on such websites is, or will remain, accurate or appropriate.

Typeset
by 4word Ltd, Bristol
Printed in Great Britain
by CPI Antony Rowe Ltd, Chippenham, Wiltshire

To Mum and Dad

Contents

List of tables   ix

1.   Leaders in conflict   1
2.   Leaders and international politics   8
3.   The emergence of the Bush doctrine   40
4.   Rumsfeld and the invasion plan   57
5.   The governance plan   68
6.   Coalition Provisional Authority   80
7.   Rumsfeld's exit strategy   94
8.   Bush takes charge   105
9.   Leadership and the Iraq war – Lessons learned   125

Appendix: Measuring the Bush and Rumsfeld worldviews using
quantitative content analysis   132

Index   136

List of tables

2.1	Number of references to advisors in Iraq policymaking books	33
3.1	Bush, Rumsfeld and the emergence of the Bush doctrine	41
4.1	Bush, Rumsfeld and the war plan	58
5.1	Bush, Rumsfeld and the governance plan	69
6.1	Coalition Provisional Authority	81
7.1	Rumsfeld's exit strategy	95
8.1	The surge	106
9.1	Bush and Iraq	128
9.2	Rumsfeld and Iraq	129
10.1	Trait scores for Rumsfeld and Bush	134

1

Leaders in conflict

When George W. Bush fired Donald H. Rumsfeld in November 2006, he ended a conflict. Not the Iraq war, which would go on for several more years, but a war about the war, fought in the shadows and engaged largely through inaction, the fudging of differences, and misdirection rather than open hostilities. In Iraq, the president was prepared to pay a high cost in American lives, treasure, and prestige to win. The secretary of defence favoured turning the war over to the Iraqis, and was comfortable with the risk that Iraq would disintegrate into chaos. With Rumsfeld removed, the president brought US strategy into line with his goals, sending additional troops to Iraq and committing to continued US involvement. Bush abandoned Secretary Rumsfeld's withdrawal approach, predicated upon the beliefs that 'it's the Iraqis' country', and 'we have to take our hand off the bicycle seat'.

Bush and Rumsfeld thought about international politics, and about leadership, in divergent ways. The president embraced binary thinking, was visceral in his commitment to the war, and had a strong belief that the US both could and should shape events in Iraq. The secretary saw the world as complex, and was sceptical of the extent of US influence over events and of the moral imperative to stay involved. They did not, of course, have stand-up fights about policy: Bush disliked disagreement, Rumsfeld was a canny courtier, and any secretary of defence openly and repeatedly confronting a president would either resign or be dismissed.[1] Bush's leadership style was to delegate, to maintain personal comity, and to be unfailingly loyal to subordinates. Rumsfeld stressed complexity and contingency, disliking grand proclamations and stating strong views. Their conflict, then, was simmering and mostly unacknowledged until the situation in Iraq was almost beyond repair. That the conflict was largely subterranean made it all the more devastating. It would have been better, for the US and for Iraqis, had the president and the secretary of defence confronted their differences much sooner than they did.

Iraq puzzles

Many paradoxes and puzzles surround US involvement in Iraq.[2] Why did the president of the United States allow a persistent disjunction between his goals and the strategy being followed by the forces under his command? Why talk of victory while the secretary of defence sought withdrawal? How could a policy of administering Iraq through a Coalition Provisional Authority be allowed to develop when it was the preference of neither the president nor the secretary of defence?

These questions are at the core of this book. I examine them as results of the clash of worldviews and decision-making styles of President Bush and Secretary Rumsfeld. I build the case that leaders matter in international politics and foreign policy decision making. Leaders differ in the way they see the world, the degree of control they believe they have over events, and their decision-making and management styles. These differences can be systematically measured and carefully traced in their impact upon policy processes and policy choices.

I seek to see the conflict through the eyes of the two principal decision makers in wartime: the president as Commander in Chief and the secretary of defence as what Eliot Cohen has termed the 'Deputy Commander in Chief'.[3] Leaders at this highest of levels fulfil two distinct functions. First, they are strategists who seek to understand the nature of the international system and the problems it generates. They develop and articulate a concept of their state, its interests, obligations, and challenges. Second, leaders at the top are administrators, charged with implementing a policy through the collection of information, effective interactions with associates and subordinates, and the management of complex organizations.

Leaders, then, develop an *external* worldview, and an *internal* management approach. Bush saw the world as one of absolutes, saw himself as a history maker, and preferred to set a general course and delegate implementation. He was averse to interpersonal conflict and saw the maintenance of optimism and morale inside his administration as a key function of leadership. Rumsfeld perceived the world as enormously complex, and saw himself, and the US, as managers rather than makers of history. He saw interpersonal conflict as productive and held in disdain those who shrank away from his probing, interrogatory style.[4]

My analysis begins with the different reactions of the president and the secretary of defence to the September 11th 2001 terrorist attacks. Bush had not thought about foreign policy in any great depth prior to this day. Reconstructing his response to the attacks allows us to track the interaction of Bush's temperament with these radically changed circumstances. Bush begins in the hours, days, weeks, and months following the attacks to outline a strategic response that was doctrinaire, ambitious, and moralizing. This set of policies became known as the Bush doctrine, and provided the rationale for the invasion of Iraq.

Rumsfeld responded differently to the attacks. He also, of course, experienced outrage – the secretary was a first responder tending to the wounded at the Pentagon. But his temperament quickly asserted itself. Whereas Bush reacted viscerally, Rumsfeld was analytical. His goal was to understand the dimensions of the new situation, and he did not want to make grand pronouncements before more was known. He disliked the notion of a war on terror, believing that it implied a vengeful and solely military response rather than a precise and multifaceted reaction. The secretary did not find it prudent to issue sweeping statements about reshaping the world.

Rumsfeld preferred the practicalities of war planning to the vagaries of grand strategy. He began a process of cajoling, interrogating, persuading, and prodding General Tommy Franks, who would command the invasion of Iraq. The secretary's goal was to produce a war plan built from new assumptions concerning force size, speed, precision, and agility. He was fully immersed in the process, and his relationship with Franks evolved from a contentious beginning to a constructive partnership.

President Bush was not deeply involved in planning for the invasion, receiving regular briefings but not asking many questions. Reassured by Rumsfeld's confidence and Franks' military bearing, Bush did not concern himself with the details. This distant and deferential relationship toward his generals held until the surge decision of late 2006.

Neither Bush nor Rumsfeld planned effectively for the governance of post-war Iraq. Both experienced some dissonance between aspects of their worldview. Bush was emotionally wed to a democratization agenda that implied the transformation of Iraqi society. Yet he had not resolved the contradiction between this and his aversion to the nation-building he associated with the Clinton era. Moreover, the president's set-the-goals but delegate-the-details management style was apparent on this issue. Bush did not thoroughly investigate the practicalities of what was going to happen on the ground after the Saddam regime was dismantled.

Rumsfeld also experienced dissonance amongst his goals. He was averse to nation-building. As a philosophical conservative, he saw enough problems with government attempts to shape society in the US, let alone abroad. Yet Rumsfeld did not trust the cadre of exiled Iraqi leaders that was the only real alternative to a US occupation. The secretary vacillated on the question of what form of government should come after Saddam, and hoped to dodge the decision.

The net result was that a compromise policy – the US would immediately stand up an Iraqi Interim Authority and oversee a rolling transfer of power – was agreed to but never implemented. Bush's inattention and Rumsfeld's vacillation allowed presidential envoy L. Paul Bremer to exercise an astonishingly broad interpretation of his instructions. He formed an instrument of occupation: the Coalition Provisional Authority (CPA). Bush's tendency to delegate and Rumsfeld's indecision ensured that a strong-willed agent – Bremer – could exercise a great degree of autonomy from his Washington-based superiors. In response, Bush bolstered Bremer's confidence rather than closely supervising him. Bremer mapped out an extensive, multi-year path to sovereignty for the Iraqis, one that proved to be more than the political and security situation in Iraq could sustain. After a year of running Iraq, the CPA was disbanded.

Rumsfeld now considered US obligations in Iraq to be at an end. His goal was to find an exit. Rumsfeld believed that the new Iraqi political process would bring greater Sunni participation. Iraqi government forces would grow more numerous and more competent. The insurgency would become a tractable problem, the Iraqis more capable, and the US less visible. Bush did not involve himself much in this strategizing. He had set the goal of a safe and democratic Iraq, and if Rumsfeld and the new commanding General George Casey said this was the means to that end, then Bush would support them.

As 2005 wore on, though, signs of success were scarce. The Sunnis remained largely outside of the now Shiite-dominated political system, and a violent minority of the Sunni community, abetted and incited by an Iraqi affiliate of the Al-Qaeda terrorist organization, continued a vicious insurgency. The problem of Shiite militias, in particular Moqtada Sadr's Mahdi army that straddled the worlds of politics and violence, remained unsolved. Rumsfeld and Casey's strategy was intended to place the US on a glide path to withdrawal, but this seemed to be an unpowered flight straight over a cliff.

In February 2006, the most holy mosque in Shiite Islam, at Samarra, was bombed by Al-Qaeda. The Shiite response, directed against their Sunni countrymen rather than US forces, was devastatingly violent. Bodies piled up in the major cities, and the country was in the midst of civil war. To Rumsfeld, this was a situation that was beyond the realm of US responsibility or capacity to rectify. He believed that the US should have left long before, and should certainly leave now. A civil war was, by definition, for the Iraqis themselves to fight.

For Bush, to leave under these circumstances was an admission of defeat. He took the most risky decision of a president in recent history. The US would not leave, scale down its goals, withdraw its forces over the horizon, or follow any other of the varieties of retreat, as Bush saw it, that were being counselled. Instead, more troops would be sent. This very personal choice – to surge troops into a situation widely regarded as beyond redemption – was a bald assertion of presidential will driven by Bush's temperament.

The core points of the study

The core points of the study are that, first and most basically, leadership matters. Bush and Rumsfeld's worldview and style shaped policy in Iraq at the key junctures. Many approaches to political science, as discussed in Chapter 2, seek to avoid close study of individual leaders and their personalities for the understandable reasons that these things are difficult to measure and sometimes of only peripheral importance to political outcomes. But, in the key episodes examined in this book, worldviews and management styles are traced to pivotal decision points, and I make the case that other individuals would have acted differently. In Iraq, and by extension in much high-level decision making on questions of war and peace, leaders are central to complete and satisfying social scientific explanation.

Second, each configuration of style and worldview brings advantages and disadvantages. This is not a story of irrational or pathological personalities, as studies of political leaders sometimes are. Bush's approach worked at some stages, such as the surge, and was disastrous at others. Rumsfeld shaped a strong invasion plan, but his hands-off approach to the post-war was in conflict with the core goals of the enterprise as envisaged by the president. Individuals, including top-level political leaders, occupy subjectively rational worlds. They do things for reasons that they consider valid at the time. Neither Bush nor Rumsfeld had an interest in creating a suboptimal strategy or a broken policymaking system. That they did so, despite their best efforts, emphasizes the importance of studying the distinctive individual characteristics of those at the top of the political system. Only by understanding how the leader saw the world, and how they sought to put their vision into action, can we understand why they did what they did.

Third, leadership is multifaceted, having both external (worldview) and internal (management style) elements, and one does not determine the other. We might expect a leader with as clear-cut an approach as Bush to be hands-on in implementing his ideas, and a leader like Rumsfeld who stresses uncertainty and complexity to be interpersonally reticent. But this was not the case. Bush had strong ideas and a weak approach to implementing them. Rumsfeld deployed a hard-charging style in service of a fairly modest worldview.

Plan of the book

In the following chapter, I seek to answer two questions: when and how are leaders important in shaping foreign policy? Which dimensions of leadership matter? I argue that leaders are significant when the environment is malleable, when they occupy a position of importance within the environment, and when they hold distinctive beliefs about what should be done. I develop a typology of leadership styles focused upon two dimensions of worldview and two of management style. In terms of worldview, *Complexity* addresses whether the leader sees the world as complex or straightforward. *History Maker vs. History Manager* addresses whether they believe they have control over what happens. In terms of management style, *Dictator or Delegator* deals with the degree of control the leader attempts to maintain over the policy process, while *Approach to Interpersonal Relations* addresses how the leader relates to advisors and other subordinates.

In the second part of Chapter 2, I develop a profile of Bush and Rumsfeld according to this typology. As noted above, Bush held a straightforward worldview and believed he was a history maker, whilst preferring a delegatory management style and a bolstering – almost cheerleading – approach to interpersonal relations. Rumsfeld saw the world as complex and had a history manager temperament, whilst he utilized a complicated management style based upon prodding and cajoling, sometimes seeming to be a bully and sometimes seeming to want to disavow responsibility for what occurred. His interpersonal approach was often brusque and sometimes interrogatory. It worked with some people, and not with others.

These profiles are presented in qualitative form in the chapter. In an appendix, I report on a quantitative analysis of the speech of Bush and Rumsfeld aimed at isolating aspects of worldview through coding spoken words. This analysis provides quantitative support for the dimensions of worldview discussed above, and readers who desire additional evidence for the portraits of Bush and Rumsfeld will find it useful. It is in an appendix in order that readers satisfied by the qualitative evidence regarding Bush and Rumsfeld's worldview can immediately move to the analysis of the policy decisions. Management style cannot be measured by content analysis of policy-related speech and so is analyzed using only qualitative methods.

Chapter 3 establishes the format for the case studies of key policy decisions in the Iraq war by displaying an overview, in table form, of how Bush and Rumsfeld's leadership characteristics shaped policymaking, and then proceeding to an in-depth analysis of how their styles mattered. In the case of the Bush doctrine, the chapter shows the dominance of President Bush's worldview, that Secretary Rumsfeld was uncomfortable with the doctrine, and therefore that the Bush doctrine is aptly named.

Chapter 4 applies this format to the planning for the military operation to remove the Saddam Hussein regime. Chapter 5 considers planning for post-war Iraq. Chapter 6 examines Bush and Rumsfeld's approach to the Coalition Provisional Authority. Chapter 7 asks why policy was allowed to drift after the disillusion of CPA, with Rumsfeld looking for an exit strategy and Bush failing to perceive the disjunction between his goals in Iraq and the strategy his defence secretary was executing. Chapter 8 details the break between Bush and Rumsfeld, as the president takes control of the war and surges troops into Iraq. Chapter 9 draws the study together, summarizing the specific elements of the Iraq decisions that were shaped by Bush and Rumsfeld as leaders, and drawing general lessons for the study of foreign policy and of leadership.

Notes

1   Compare, for example, the conflict analyzed here with the experiences of Robert McNamara and McGeorge Bundy, both of whom fudged differences with President Lyndon Johnson on the escalation of the Vietnam War, feeling that first loyalty, and then indirect opposition to the president, represented the only available strategies at their disposal. Both departed the administration soon after President Johnson became fully cognizant of the differences between their views and his own. See H.R. McMaster, *Dereliction of Duty: Johnson, McNamara, the Joint Chiefs of Staff and the Lies that Lead to Vietnam* (New York: Harper, 1998); and Gordon M. Goldstein, *Lessons in Disaster: McGeorge Bundy and the Path to War in Vietnam* (New York: Holt, 2009).

2 This continued to be the case in the administration of President Bush's successor, Barack Obama. See Michael R. Gordon, 'In US Exit from Iraq: Failed Efforts and Challenges'. *New York Times*, 24 September 2012. Available at www.nytimes.com/2012/09/23/world/ middleeast/failed-efforts-of-americas-last-months-in-iraq.html. A fruitful area of future research will be a comparative study of the decision-making style and strategic principles of Bush and Obama on both Iraq and Afghanistan, two conflicts Obama inherited from Bush and upon which both made decisions of tremendous importance.

3 C-SPAN, 'Q & A with Eliot Cohen', 21 July 2005. Accessed 17 October 2010. www.c-spanvideo.org/program/187812-1.

4 Bush and Rumsfeld as individuals excite high – and amongst academic observers usually negative – emotions (see, for example, the survey at: www.foreignpolicy.com/articles/2012/01/03/the_ivory_tower?page=0,6). It is important to stress at the outset that I seek to analyze their worldviews and decision styles and consider how they shaped the major decisions in the Iraq war, rather than to indict or vindicate them as individuals. The question I hope to prompt in the reader's mind is not 'is this pro or anti Bush/Rumsfeld?' Rather, the relevant question is 'were these individuals important to what happened, and would matters have unfolded in a different way with a different president/secretary of defence?'

2

Leaders and international politics

In this chapter, I seek to answer crucial questions: when and how do leaders matter in shaping a state's foreign policy? Which dimensions of leadership are important? I then offer a portrait of Bush and Rumsfeld as leaders, utilizing multiple sources of evidence to understand their worldviews and management styles. Readers less concerned with matters of political science and more concerned with Bush, Rumsfeld, and Iraq, can move to Chapter 3 without significant loss of understanding.

There are two affirmative statements about the importance of leaders in shaping foreign policy that we should consider: *leaders always matter* and *leaders sometimes matter*. In the former, leaders are seen as *causal mechanisms:* components of systems that transmit causal force between an input such as a strategic imperative, and an output such as the action of a state.[1] In the latter, we regard leaders as *causal variables*, interacting with material and ideational forces as explanatory factors accounting for state action.

I subscribe to the position that leaders *always* matter in the sense of their actions always being necessary for the state to do anything (leaders as causal mechanisms), but the really interesting cases are where different leaders, in similar situations, do or want to do different things (leaders as causal variables). The argument of the book is that Bush and Rumsfeld were different types of leaders, they wanted to do different things in Iraq, and this is crucial in understanding US policy.

We should first consider the argument that *leaders always matter.* Individuals in executive positions at the top of their state serve, in this reading, as the locus of integration for the material and ideational factors that bear upon a state's options and actions. When international relations theorists talk about 'the state' as doing or thinking something, they are engaging in shorthand, personifying for convenience an entity that, when considered literally, is incapable of doing or thinking anything. The state, then, is its decision makers.[2] These decision makers perceive the situation they are in, consider options, choose, and implement. Some schools of thought argue or implicitly assume that individual leaders do this in uniform ways and so are largely interchangeable. This is the position, most obviously, of rational choice theory. Realism, especially the newer 'neo-classical' variant, pays some attention to individual differences. But most theories of international politics subscribe to the assumption that leaders are basically the same, and if we understand the imperatives of the situation they are in, we can understand why they act as they do. Constructivists at first glance seem amenable to the influence of leadership, as their opening gambit is that material factors are indeterminate causes of outcomes. Yet, for the most part, constructivisms seek to focus on 'collectively held' ideas along the lines of 'the UK's self-image as a post-imperial power' rather than upon variation in the individual beliefs of decision makers.

In this line of thinking, then, leaders need not be studied by political scientists as the goal is to model the essential parts of reality, rather than describe every detail. Yet, not even the strictest proponent of IR theory would deny that leaders are important in transmitting the causal force of material or ideational variables into state action. They would just say that since any leader would respond to the material or ideational environment in broadly the same way, leadership variance is negligible and so there is little to be gained – and much loss of parsimony – by including leaders in the causal model.[3]

What if leaders do not always transform material and ideational stimuli into action in identical or even similar ways? If political leaders have idiosyncratic belief systems, personalities, and past experiences – in other words, if political leaders are like all other human beings on the planet – then the choices they make will be the most interesting part of international affairs. If leaders are not interchangeable, then we need to understand the differences between them. In this line of argument, failing to take leaders into account results in incomplete explanations of foreign policy. Grand international relations theories may do well in explaining broad patterns of outcomes across international systems and over large numbers of years, but explanation of specific state actions will often require investigation into policy actors and processes. Sometimes material and ideational factors will present such compelling incentives for and against courses of action that leaders will indeed respond in largely uniform ways.[4] Yet sometimes material and ideational incentives will be weaker, or the subjective construction of the meaning of these incentives by the leader will be very strong, and who leads will matter. Leaders then become more than causal *mechanisms*; they become causal *variables* in their own right.

In the first position, leaders *always* matter, but in causally trivial ways as mere automatic mechanisms for transferring material and ideational forces into state action. In this second view, leaders *sometimes* matter, but when they do, they are crucial in determining what the state does and what processes lead to this action. Leaders become shapers, rather than mere mirrors, of their environment.[5] When will leaders shape, and not just reflect, their circumstances?[6]

Two further questions can sharpen our thinking.[7] We should first ask: *if the leader is removed from the situation, would the outcome change?* This is a matter of placement within the environment, and of the malleability of the situation. Is the leader in a position to shape events, and is the situation fluid enough to be shaped? If I lead a small state within an international system dominated by great powers – say, Cuba during the Cold War – most actions that I take will not massively alter the course of world history. If, though, I am the leader of a superpower, then my actions are much more likely to be consequential. Or if the superpowers find themselves in direct confrontation over happenings within my small state – as the United States and the Soviet Union did in October 1962 over the placement of Soviet nuclear weapons on Cuba – then my actions as leader of a small state could be the hinge upon which rests the fate of the world. The same leader – in this case, Cuban President Fidel Castro – can be seen as less central to the broad sweep of superpower history during much of his time in office but entirely crucial for the specific period of the Cuban Missile Crisis. Moreover, if the research question is changed from what explains the broad contours of great power politics to what explains the foreign policy of Cuba, then Castro's placement within the relevant environment is suddenly more central. Whilst it would be reductionist to explain the entirety of the Cold War by studying Castro's worldview, it would be absurd to explain the Cuban Missile Crisis, Cuban foreign policy, or interactions between Cuba and the superpowers without doing so.[8]

The malleability of the situation also affects the scope for influence by leaders. If the situation is highly structured then what any individual does is unlikely to change history. Once the United States entered the Second World War on the allied side, for example, most courses of action open to Adolf Hitler would have resulted in German defeat. His decisions could hasten or forestall the defeat, but the blunt fact of allied victory was, as Winston Churchill put it, merely a matter of 'the proper application of overwhelming force'.[9] If, though, the situation is fluid or novel, then individual action has greater scope to shape outcomes.

Environmental placement and malleability are the components of what Fred I. Greenstein terms *action indispensability*: the actions of a strategically placed individual in a malleable situation are more likely to be indispensable to (necessary causes of) an outcome than the actions of an individual on the periphery of events within a heavily structured setting.[10]

A second question to ask is *whether any individual, put in the same situation, would take the same actions?* A choice can be so obvious that it is hard to imagine anyone taking a different course. This is sometimes a matter of compelling circumstances combined with the basic rationality of the human species (when a room is on fire, we all run for the exit), sometimes a matter of individuals being drawn from common cultural and historical reference points, and sometimes both. No British prime minister, for example, will take office and immediately declare war upon the United States, for reasons both of rational self-interest (the British would lose) and cultural commonality (the UK and the US are friends).

However, many situations are sufficiently ambiguous that different individuals would make different choices. Tony Blair, for example, had a distinct set of beliefs about the world and about the alliance with the United States. He supported the US in Iraq, where many others who could have taken his place would have made a different choice.[11] This is Greenstein's concept of *actor indispensability* – are the specific characteristics and beliefs of the leader necessary causes of (indispensable to) the choices that individual makes, or would anyone in that position do the same thing? If we ask questions about highly structured situations and we are interested in non-controversial courses of action – not declaring war on your superpower ally, for example – then the personality and beliefs of an individual leader are not major causal factors. If, though, we ask about fluid situations and courses of action about which reasonable people disagree – such as supporting your superpower ally in a war of choice opposed by a majority of your population – then the leader looms large as a worthwhile topic of investigation.

We must ask, then, *if this leader had not been in office, how would events have differed? Would anyone, faced with these circumstances, have done what this leader did?* Considering these questions can carve out for us justifications for considering political leadership as causally crucial under certain circumstances. But what aspects of political leadership matter? How do political leaders differ from one another in ways that can impact policy process and policy choice and so shape state foreign policy and – ultimately – international outcomes?

Worldview and management style: dimensions of leadership

Understanding the linkage between politicians' personalities and their policy choices has proven challenging for political scientists. Two difficulties recur – developing conceptualizations of individual characteristics that allow for differentiation between individuals yet are broad enough to permit comparison across individuals; and the related challenge of measuring personality in ways that are reliable and non-tautological (i.e. not merely inferring policy beliefs from policy choices).[12]

Early attempts to link personality to policy were heavily influenced by the depth psychology associated with Sigmund Freud. The cornerstone of this approach was that personality was essentially determined in early life by interactions with the mother and father, and focused upon the related drives of aggression and sexuality. This approach was made explicitly relevant to political leadership by Harold Lasswell, who posited that behaviour was essentially the projection of private needs upon public objects.[13] The US government, in the first attempts to utilize personality profiles of adversaries to formulate government policy, commissioned studies of Adolf Hitler that traced his expansionist policies to his damaged sense of self, and accurately predicted his suicide as Germany faced its final defeat.[14] In political science and history, this approach became known as 'psychobiography', and reached its highpoint in the magisterial study of Woodrow Wilson by Alexander and Juliette George, which traced Wilson's consistent inability to compromise in order to achieve his political goals to his fraught relationship with a domineering father.[15]

Psychobiography has a long and distinguished history and, in modified forms, retains adherents today.[16] It has sometimes proven difficult, though, to trace a clear causal line between early life experiences and differing policy preferences on the political issues of the day. Moreover, the psychoanalytic underpinnings of the approach determined that the focus would be on abnormalities of personality, and abnormal political figures, leading to the derisive label of 'patho-biography'. The method seemed less well suited to understanding political figures who fell within a more normal spectrum of personality and behaviour.

Subsequent developments in psychology shifted attention away from early life experience and from unconscious, private drives projected onto public life. The 'cognitive revolution' – the understanding that all human beings engage in theory-driven information processing that determines what they see, what the recall, what lessons of the past they apply to the present, and what action scripts drive their behaviour, swept through the study of political leadership.[17] Political beliefs – what is the nature of the political universe? How much control can I have over political life? – became and have remained a fruitful focus of study.[18]

Studying normal personality configurations led to a focus upon relatively stable traits – recurrent approaches to the political environment – as a core facet of political identity. After a long debate, psychologists now believe that some stable personality characteristics run through an adult life, although the way in which they shape behaviour is complex and varies by situation.[19]

The core challenges for modern personality and cognitive approaches to political leadership, then, are to study facets of psychology that have clear linkages to political choice without simply being circular (i.e. relabelling a political choice as a personality characteristic and then stating that the characteristic caused the choice), and in measuring those facets of individual approach in reliable ways.[20]

In regard to the measurement challenge, in this study of Bush and Rumsfeld I adopt a multi-method approach, relying upon a qualitative account of personality drawn from original interviews and secondary sources and a quantitative content analysis of leaders' speech (see Appendix). In dealing with the conceptual challenge, I draw upon two facets of worldview that are traits of especial importance to foreign policy: the complexity of their worldview and the degree to which they believe they can shape events. I then draw two dimensions of management style from the literature on elite political decision making: degree of preferred control over policy process and approach to interpersonal relations.

Worldviews: complexity and control

The first dimension of worldview is the degree of complexity in the political leader's view of the world.[21] Does the leader see nuance, detail and contingency, or certainty, bold facts and moral absolutes? Are they given to emotional responses or an analytical approach? Individuals with a less complex worldview see politics as essentially divided into clear categories: friends and enemies, good and evil. They are comfortable with absolutes, require less information prior to making decisions, and are less apt to examine the underlying assumptions of policy or to revisit policy decisions once made.

Leaders with a more complex worldview, by contrast, see many shades of grey in the political world. They see human behaviour and political life as complex, multi-causal, and rarely best understood or responded to with absolute and inflexible policies. They exhibit especial interest in understanding the many sides of an issue or a decision, and are much more likely to reconsider both strategy and tactics as new information arrives.

Ronald Reagan had a monochromatic worldview, focused on good and evil. He saw the world as straightforward and insisted that internal policy discussion be focused upon core principles.[22] Barack Obama, by contrast, sees the world as complex and prefers a case-by-case policy approach. In foreign policy, he some-times seemed to be a realist, drawn to a hard-nosed power politics approach. On other occasions he seemed to be an idealist, seeking to alter the internal politics of states in a democratic direction. This flexibility is characteristic of those with nuanced worldviews.[23] This dimension of leadership is captured in the apho-rism of the Fox, who knows many things and the Hedgehog, who knows one big thing. Worldview complexity is conceptualized as a relatively stable personality trait that is consistent with a wide variety of more specific political ideologies and beliefs.[24] One can be a conservative who sees the world as complex or simple, and a dogmatic or a pragmatic liberal. There is no conceptual link (and little evidence of an empirical one) between complexity and intelligence. Nor does high complexity necessarily lead to superior analysis and choice. Whether a high or low complex-ity leader has the better approach depends upon the issue at hand – for example, Neville Chamberlain's nuanced view of Adolf Hitler led him to follow a policy of negotiation and appeasement, whilst Winston Churchill's relentlessly monochro-matic view of the situation allowed him to perceive the Nazi implacability earlier than many of his peers.

A second key dimension of worldview focuses upon the degree of control the leader perceives they have over their political environment and, to put it most grandly, the course of history. This is a core political belief concerning whether one can shape history, reconfiguring one's environment through bold and decisive action, or whether the proper approach is to react, nudge, and manage environmen-tal forces, with radical changes of circumstances coming from forces beyond the command of any individual or state. Is one, to utilize a conceptual scheme formu-lated by Henry Kissinger, a revolutionary statesperson or a conservative? Kissinger, fearing revolutions as a source of instability, revered those practitioners of diplo-macy who managed the tides of history and promoted stability.[25] Alexander L. George suggested that whether a statesperson believes they can exercise 'control and mastery' over historical development, and whether they can 'move and shape' history in the desired direction, was a key part of their approach to political life.[26]

One of the central debates over leadership has been whether great leaders change history or history changes common individuals into great leaders.[27] Is it the person, or the times? This question is unanswerable in the abstract, but taps an important dimension of an individual's approach to the world. History maker versus history manager – the labels I have given to this dimension of worldview – refers to a belief about control over the environment, rather than the objective fact of such control.[28]

George H.W. Bush, for example, thought that the role of a great power like the United States was to manage chaos within the international system. He was cautious about becoming involved in world historical change, in particular the revolutions of 1989–1990 that swept aside the Soviet Union and seemed poised to do the same to the Chinese communist regime. Bush wanted to ensure that the violence and negative consequences of instability were mitigated. On assuming the presidency from Ronald Reagan, Bush instituted a year-long pause in negotiations between the United States and the Soviet Union and, later, he clung to Gorbachev's Soviet regime rather than embracing the Russian democratic movement of Boris Yeltsin.[29] The contrast with Reagan, who had instigated a radical transformation of the US-Soviet relationship, was stark. Reagan believed in making history; Bush believed in managing it.

As with complexity of worldview, different beliefs about historical control are not meant as proxies for intelligence or, on their own, as likely to lead to better or worse outcomes. The leader may misperceive how much control they have over events. A false belief that one can only be reactive might lead to missed opportunities to reshape the environment in advantageous ways, whereas a false belief in the ability to shape history can lead to hubris and overreach.

These two dimensions – complexity of worldview and belief in control over the environment – represent core dimensions of worldview that are precise enough to allow for differentiation between political leaders and yet not so narrow as to be essentially a relabelling of policy choice on specific issues. Worldview, defined as complexity and control, is the external side of political leadership. Yet high-level political figures must also develop a policymaking style, and it is to this 'internal' sphere of leadership that I now turn, examining management styles and approaches to interpersonal relations between leaders and advisors as shapers of policy process and choice.[30]

Management style: control of process and interpersonal relations

The literature on organizational aspects of decision making focuses on both formal processes and informal interactions. Both work in combination to determine the shape of policymaking. It is important to understand these characteristic patterns of policymaking in order to place the Bush/Rumsfeld interaction in context.

Most work on advisory systems begins with three classic models developed by Richard Tanner Johnson.[31] The *competitive* model involves advisors given ambiguous and overlapping roles within a context of managed organizational chaos. Subordinates compete for the favour of the president, who benefits from a marketplace of ideas and the resulting energy and original thinking. This requires a president who is heavily engaged and comfortable with conflict amongst advisors. President Franklin D. Roosevelt set up the archetypal version of this system.[32]

A second classic model is the *formalistic* type. This hierarchical structure is based upon clearly delineated roles. Policymaking proceeds through structured channels within departments and agencies, with policy papers and memoranda (these are preferred to verbal free-thinking) delivered up a defined chain of command. Formalistic systems often involve a gatekeeper, usually the chief of staff or national security advisor, reviewing the policy options before they go, often with the gatekeeper's recommendation affixed, to the president. A choice is made, and then passed back down the chain of command for implementation. Formalistic systems have the strength of preserving the president's time and energies for the key decisions, and promoting orderly governance. The downside is that the president can be presented with options separate from the context and discussion that generated them, can miss the opportunity to push for alternative options early in the policy process, and the system can be slow-moving and lack the capacity for innovation. President Dwight D. Eisenhower employed a pure formalistic system, and Richard Nixon also preferred a formalistic policymaking process.[33]

The final of Johnson's three archetypes is the *collegial* system. As an archetype, this system involves the president in deliberations at all stages of the policy process, collecting together advisors from several ranks of the bureaucracy and having free-wheeling discussions, with options emerging from brainstorming sessions. It relies upon good relationships amongst advisors in order to facilitate free exchange, and a president who is comfortable with intellectual debate, does not require consensus from advisors, and is intellectually agile and knowledgeable so as to be able to hold his own in policy discussion. The advantages can be a tremendous exchange of information, ideas, and perspectives both vertically and horizontally within the policymaking system, with the president understanding the full context of policy debate. The downsides can be a potentially disorderly process, good at generating ideas but bad at crafting precise options, and the demands on the intellectual and emotional intelligence of the president make it unsuitable for every chief executive. John F. Kennedy ran a collegial system.[34]

Johnson's models are of enduring value in understanding presidential policymaking systems, prompting key questions of how much leaders want to control process and how comfortable they are with debate and conflict. Johnson's models have been criticized, though, for being both too few and too static. Those studying advisory systems since Johnson have stressed that presidents can adopt a variety of advisory arrangements over time and when working on different issues.[35] Patrick J. Haney found it useful to develop hybrid categories, such as Formalistic-Competitive, and Collegial-Formalistic, as he examined the empirical evidence on decision making during foreign policy crises.[36] But whatever their limitations when taken as rigid categories, Johnson's models do contain essential truths about core differences between presidencies, and so – as heuristics – are of worth.[37] Moreover, whilst Johnson's work is often reduced in review to a table of bullet points showing the key points of each model, the studies of each system in operation that comprise the bulk of *Managing the White House* are nuanced and based upon a core point of great relevance to this study: the formal structure of the model is less important than the personal characteristics of the president who is managing it. The style of the president is of key importance to which model he will institute and how that model will function in practice.[38]

Alexander George took Johnson's models and added components of presidential personality – *cognitive style*, *sense of efficacy and competence*, and *orientation toward political conflict*. These factors of style, George argues, 'will shape the formal structure of the policymaking system that [the president] creates around himself and, even more, will influence the ways in which he encourages and permits that formal structure to operate in practice.'[39] A president, Meena Bose concurs, 'must adopt a decision-making style that fits with his personality'.[40] Colin Powell, asked directly about the policymaking system in the first Bush term, said it was 'a manifestation of the personality of the president, the kind of system he wanted to have'.[41]

In addition to the formal models, then, the informal dynamics of interactions amongst presidents and advisors must be considered. Richard Tanner Johnson was acutely aware of this. Tanner Johnson writes that President Lyndon B. Johnson, for example, wanted to institute a formal system but constantly worked against it in practice by picking up the phone and talking to aides directly, or drawing upon ad hoc groups – such as his famous Tuesday lunch group on Vietnam – for advice and support. He recognized the value of formal advice but didn't have the patience to work through the system he created. 'The core of the problem was [President] Johnson himself: his personality repeatedly overshadowed his management system. While Johnson gravitated toward a more-or-less orderly formalistic type managerial system, his personal style frequently disrupted his staff and the system he sought to institute.'[42]

Finally, a gap in our understanding of these systems – and a key purpose of this book is to address this gap – has been in studying the impact of the personalities of predominant advisors within the system. Work on advisory systems has tended, at least implicitly, to view advisors as essentially pawns to be positioned and arranged by the president. But, just as presidential style is important, so is the personality of key advisors. As David Rothkopf puts it, 'of the few serious tomes written about the national security apparatus of the United States, there is vastly too much focus on policy and process and too little on people, their work culture, their philosophies, the psychology of the interaction.'[43] The operation of a policy system in practice will depend on the mix of personalities that operate within it. Policymaking on Iraq, to reiterate the core contention of this book, was shaped not solely by President Bush's beliefs and style, but by the collision of these with Secretary Rumsfeld's very different approach.

Two core dimensions of policy style that emerge from these literatures are degree of control preferred by the leaders, and approach to interpersonal relations. Is the leader a director or a delegator? Do they prefer to tightly control decisions from the point of inception to execution, or are they happy setting a broad course and allowing others to carry policies forward? Leadership can be commanding, with the leader closely involved in all aspects of the policymaking process, dominating debate, and keeping a close watch over implementation. Or a leader can be content, believing it most efficient, to set broad goals and then delegate the detailed work to subordinates.[44] Leaders utilizing a collegial or competitive model are more deeply involved in policy generation, debate, and implementation than leaders using a formalistic model. To give some examples, Ronald Reagan was reliant upon advisors to implement his wishes. He specified destinations, and left it to subordinates to map out the route.[45] By contrast, Reagan's predecessor Jimmy Carter directed policy from the generation of options to the final execution. Carter believed the key to good decision making was immersion in detail and the constant personal involvement of the chief executive.[46]

Finally, how do leaders approach interpersonal relations? Are they averse to conflict with colleagues and subordinates? Do they see their role as maintaining a focus on tasks or on harmonious interactions? Some leaders find conflict – the open airing of disagreements, an adversarial atmosphere, and competition for the leader's ear – to be the best way to ask hard questions and compel the optimal performance from subordinates. Other leaders find this uncomfortable or self-defeating. They prefer a harmonious consensus, and see their role as bolstering morale.[47] Some presidents enjoy and thrive upon the dirty business of politics, whether within or without their administration, whilst others prefer to transcend division, finding it unhelpful or distasteful. The collegial model of policymaking does not function well in the presence of interpersonal divisions, and the formalistic model is explicitly designed to remove conflict from the process and to shield the president from manifestations of it. By contrast, the competitive system is intended to actively promote conflict and requires that a president employing it be both comfortable and skilled in turning rancour to productive ends.

Franklin D. Roosevelt saw competition between advisors as beneficial and deliberately gave overlapping assignments and drew ambiguous boundaries of authority in order to promote it. In a competitive atmosphere, Roosevelt believed, individuals would raise their level of performance and superior ideas would win out. By contrast, Richard M. Nixon found interpersonal conflict uncomfortable, and did not trust his temper in the heat of debate. He sought to keep face-to-face conflict to a minimum and made decisions using options papers.[48] Barack Obama, whilst more confident in interpersonal terms than Nixon, disliked conflict amongst advisors, finding it jarred with his preferred deliberative, emotionally cool decision-making style.[49]

I turn now to portraits of Bush and Rumsfeld on the four dimensions of leadership developed above. I construct the profiles from interviews with their associates, documents, and the secondary literature. In terms of complexity and control – the *worldview* element of leadership – the approach is multi-method. The Appendix details a quantitative content analysis that captures significant and stable differences in the way Bush and Rumsfeld talked about, and by inference thought about, the complexity and malleability of political life. Management style is much harder to infer from quantitative content analysis and so the analysis on the *internal* element of leadership is purely qualitative.

A portrait of two leaders

Bush's worldview and management style

Black-and-white worldview

Early in his presidency, George W. Bush was asked by a student at an elementary school whether he found decision making difficult:

> Not really. If you know what you believe, decisions come pretty easy. If you're one of those types of people that are always trying to figure out which way the wind is blowing, decision making can be difficult. But…I know who I am. I know what I believe in, and I know where I want to lead the country.[50]

The distinctive feature of Bush's leadership was his Manichean, black-and-white worldview, and associated traits: a focus upon a limited number of core goals, reluctance to reconsider policies and courses of action once they had been decided upon, moral certainty, and visceral, emotional reactions. President Bush disliked second-guessing policy decisions, famously preferred decision making based on fundamental principles rather than near-term considerations, and was comfortable operating upon core instincts.[51] 'I'm a gut player' was one of several iconic self-descriptions.[52]

Former British Prime Minister Tony Blair has a good claim to be amongst those who best understood the president. Bush wrote in his memoirs that he and Blair had 'the closest friendship I would form with any foreign leader.'[53] Blair is incisive on the subject of Bush's certainty – perhaps because his own worldview was similar:[54]

> [T]o succeed in US politics, or that of the UK, you have to be more than clever. You have to be able to connect and you have to be able to articulate that connection in plain

language. The plainness of the language then leads people to look past the brainpower involved…sometimes the plainness touches something else: A simplicity that is the product of a decisive nature…George had immense simplicity in how he saw the world. Right or wrong, it led to decisive leadership. Now you may disagree strongly with the decisions, but the opposite also has its problems.[55]

Bush disliked self-reflection. His biographer Robert Draper sought to draw the president into a conversation of this type, and encountered a stone wall: 'You're the observer. I'm not. I really do not feel comfortable in the role of analyzing myself. I'll *try*.'[56] Bush's former press secretary Scott McClellan reached a similar conclusion: 'Bush was not one to look back once a decision was made. Rather than suffer any sense of guilt and anguish, Bush chose not to go down the road of self-doubt.'[57] David Kay, the Iraq weapons inspector, spent a lot of time with the president whilst he was making very significant decisions:

> He has a tremendous sense of calm and certitude about the positions he takes, and is unusually doubt-free about them. Most people, when they make monumental decisions, understand that they're doing it under conditions of great uncertainty, and are not fully at the time really able to understand what the consequences might be – and that frightens them, or at least they have concern, disquietude about it. This president has none of that, as far as I can tell.[58]

A worldview of certainty begets great conviction and stubbornness, a facet of Bush's temperament that was readily apparent.[59] 'He does not second-guess himself about decisions', says Tom Schieffer, who worked with Bush during the time he was co-owner of the Texas Rangers major league baseball franchise. 'George is very good at addressing problems as they come across his desk and then moving on to the next one. When he makes mistakes, he doesn't dwell on them, he tries to learn from them. He thinks it's important to be decisive and provide some leadership.'[60] As the president himself put it to his biographer Robert Draper, 'If you're weak internally, this job will run you all over town.'[61]

Peter Feaver, a former National Security Council staffer, confirmed this picture of the president: 'He is very strong, not dissuaded by *New York Times* editorials, bad public opinion polls, if he has thought a matter through and thinks he's doing the right thing, by golly he'll do it no matter what people say, certainly what certain kinds of people say like the *New York Times* editorial page, or certain academics.'[62]

As Bush told Draper:

> When you're responsible for putting a kid in harm's way, you better understand that if that kid thinks you're making a decision based on polls – or something other than what you think is right, or wrong, or based upon principles – then you're letting that kid down. *And* you're creating conditions for doubt. And you can't give a kid a gun and have him doubt whether or not he's gonna be supported in all ways. And you can't learn that until you're the guy sitting behind the desk.[63]

Bush possessed a striking moral certainty. The president would often speak in terms of absolute good and absolute evil. He was comfortable with grand, teleological constructs that posited absolute truths. Accompanying this was an emotional reaction to politics and to historical events. This comes, at least partly, from Bush's reading of his faith. In an insightful portrait, journalist Richard Brookhiser discussed the issue with former House Speaker Newt Gingrich, speechwriter David Frum, and former Indiana Governor Mitch Daniels:

> Bush's faith makes 'his sense of history very hard for secular intellectuals to understand,' according to Gingrich. 'The great mystery in his decision-making,' Frum says, 'is the role of religion. When Bush says, I'll pray on this, it's not a figure of speech.' Mitchell Daniels believes that faith gives Bush 'a certain serenity,' as if he trusts that 'history will take care of itself if he pursues the right policies.' Practically, Bush's faith means that he does not tolerate, or even recognize, ambiguity: there is an all-knowing God who decrees certain behaviors, and leaders must obey.[64]

A Bush family friend agrees that this was an important factor in President Bush's worldview: 'You have to look at the president and religion...I don't know exactly what it means to be a born-again Christian but, if it means that Jesus has entered your soul, then does it mean that you are infallible? I don't know the answer to that. But it may impart a certitude to the president that affects the way he reacts to his team and everything else.'[65]

History maker

Bush saw history as amenable to control if one was prepared to act boldly, accept risk, and stay the course.[66] As David Frum noted in 2003, 'at every important juncture of the war on terror, he [has] opted for the high-risk option.'[67] Joshua Muravchik concurs that 'to use a metaphor from the sport in which Bush worked before turning to politics...he will be recalled as a big swinger who belted his share of home runs but also struck out too many times to be voted into the Hall of Fame.'[68] Peter Wehner, the White House director of strategic initiatives from 2002–2007, says:

> He has always viewed the presidency in those terms...the sense that you get one bite at the apple to do it. And he is by disposition and temperament someone who wants to shape history and bend it in certain ways. I don't know if it's a product of his upbringing, or just a product of how one is hardwired, a certain view toward life, a certain capacity for rolling the dice, a certain willingness to dare, and to take chances, to advance causes you believe in. So it's a character issue, and I suspect like so many areas of character it's a complicated mix of nature and nurture.[69]

Bill Keller, in an influential comparison of Bush and Ronald Reagan, concluded that 'each man will be remembered as a risk-taker. They each have an impulse for the audacious.' Keller wrote, 'If [Bush] fails, my guess is that it will be a failure not of caution but of overreaching, which means it will be failure on a grand scale.'[70] As Bush told Robert Draper, risk-taking has to be accompanied by confidence. 'The other thing is that *you can't fake it.* You have to believe it. And I believe it. I believe we'll succeed.'[71] Optimism, Draper concluded:

[W]as basic to Bush. Disgruntlements did not fester; failure was not a thing to fear. Bush could push through crises – alcohol abuse, defeat in New Hampshire, thousands killed in the homeland on his watch – with little in the way of self-doubt or residual gloom. Bush liked to say that the unconditional love of his parents and religious faith were his props. The more cynical assessment was that the privileged son of George Herbert Walker Bush could afford to roll the dice.[72]

Delegator

Delegation as an approach to management was ingrained in Bush prior to his assumption of the presidency. Much biographical work traces the tendency to his study of executive practice at Harvard Business School, and sees the style at work in his business ventures and governorship of Texas.[73] Bush felt his MBA taught him 'the importance of setting clear goals for an organization, delegating tasks, and holding people to account.'[74] An associate from his time at the Texas Rangers recalls that 'He very much believes that the chief executive's responsibility is to manage the other executives.'[75] Robert Draper concurs that 'among George W.'s lifelong attributes were his awareness of his own limits and the willingness to surround himself with able (though loyal!) experts.'[76]

The president disliked paperwork in general, although perhaps not to the degree to which Lawrence Wilkerson, Colin Powell's chief of staff, claims: 'I doubt whether he has read 200 pages in his life.'[77] Franklin Miller, of the National Security Council staff, often briefed the president. 'PowerPoint worked with him. I think long, involved, convoluted briefings didn't work with him. As with many senior decision makers, he had a limited time budget, with lots of other things on his mind. 40 or 50 slides that get down into the weeds level [we]re inappropriate and self-defeating.'[78]

Rather than relying upon written work, Bush preferred to understand the person with whom he was dealing. If he was comfortable with a person then he trusted the accuracy of their information and the quality of their judgement without much further investigation. Donald Rumsfeld, in one of the very few comments in his memoir on the president's style, wrote 'I found Bush incisive. He showed insight into human character and, I found, often had an impressive read of the nature and intentions of foreign officials.'[79] As Scott McClellan puts it, Bush 'often speaks about the people he likes in terms of their inner character – a good man, a decent man – rather than in terms of their concrete behaviors and actions.' The president quite famously used this technique upon meeting Vladimir Putin, focusing upon Putin's wearing of a cross as an indication of shared values.[80]

Interpersonal style

Bush disliked confrontation, and saw his role as bolstering and providing confidence to subordinates. As Bush put it to Bob Woodward, 'A president has got to be the calcium in the backbone.'[81] This could, on occasion, be troublesome – if Bush liked the bearing of the individual, did not inquire much into what they said, and gave them a presidential pat on the back, subpar performance would go uncorrected. However, the style also had benefits, and could inspire loyalty from subordinates.[82] Eliot Cohen, a distinguished student of wartime leadership who served in the Bush administration during the second term, comments:

> [H]e clearly felt that it was his job to keep people's morale up, and to instil a sense that – the administration is getting a lot of abuse from many quarters – but just keep your chin up, and do your duty, and don't worry about it, and let the historians have their say about it. He was very effective at communicating that throughout the system. He clearly thought that his job was often to give other people backbone.[83]

Rumsfeld's worldview and management style

Nuanced worldview

If the leitmotif of Bush's worldview was certainty, the theme of Rumsfeld's was nuance and contingency. Douglas Feith noted:

> Despite a common misperception, Rumsfeld was not closed-minded or ideological. Indeed, he was actively anti-ideological: All ideas, theories and preconceptions were open to continual examination and challenge…This continual process of evaluation was the most significant feature of Rumsfeld's mind – though many failed to recognize it, perhaps because they could not see past his intimidating personality.[84]

One of the secretary's favourite axioms, Feith reports, was 'When you can't solve a problem, expand it.'[85] Lawrence Di Rita, one of Rumsfeld's closest aides, confirms this approach:

> He is not somebody who tends to see things in clear, black-and-white, yes-and-no, go-no go terms. He has been around long enough, and he has a natural skepticism of things he hears and things he is told, and so he is constantly challenging and refreshing his knowledge of stuff. He has strong beliefs and a clear political philosophy but in his approach to policy making and to the globe, he is not an ideologue in that sense.[86]

This should not be overstated. Rumsfeld, as Di Rita notes, did hold strong beliefs which he did not change, such as the necessity of a transformational approach to the military and the belief that democratization, and long-term involvement in Iraq, were not appropriate US goals. Yet both of these beliefs had their root in Rumsfeld's complex view of the world. As discussed in Chapter 4, transformation was a doctrine he embraced as a challenge to what he perceived as stale thinking and unexamined assumptions in the armed forces. Democratization, again as discussed below, was something Rumsfeld saw as a simplistic slogan that would in practice prove to be far more complex than its proponents believed. Many have missed the nuance in Rumsfeld's approach to the world. Making it a focus in this book generates significant new insight on the major Iraq decisions.

Associates found that Rumsfeld stressed uncertainty as a strategic principle. '[O]fficials' he wrote '[n]eed to periodically reexamine their own views and judgments. Human beings are fallible, and the information policy makers use to make their judgments is always incomplete, imperfect, and ever changing. The assumptions that underlie strategy can become stale or even proven wrong to begin with.'[87] Thomas White, the former secretary of the army, saw him as 'a pragmatist...He has certain things he wants to get done...I never viewed him as an ideologue, the way I would characterize Paul Wolfowitz.'[88] For Douglas Feith, Rumsfeld had a 'toolbox approach...never to approach problems with only a hammer because life is complex and not all problems are nails.'[89]

This approach to the world at the macro level had clear consequences for the way that Rumsfeld made decisions and it is important to make the link. For an individual with a highly complex worldview, stressing uncertainty and pragmatism, the process often *is* the policy. Consistent with this, Rumsfeld disliked being faced with finished work and making grand choices. He wanted to participate in the development of options, and for these options to be derived from a rigorous understanding of the problem and the assumptions that were being made. Gordon England, who succeeded Paul Wolfowitz as deputy secretary of defence, said of Rumsfeld:

> He is a very analytically based decision maker, not sort of the broadest. His approach was more based on data, facts, and analysis, so decisions always involved a lot of hard work leading up to them. That's different than a lot of senior executives who sort of assimilate things, have a lot of sense about things and make broad-based decisions.[90]

One senior executive who made broad-based decisions, of course, was President Bush. Rumsfeld's view of decision making was very different than Bush's clear-cut, stand-and-deliver style. Rumsfeld characterized the process:

> What happens is discussion takes place, pros and cons are considered and we [the president's advisors] participate in those. The president then begins leaning in a direction [and] people say, well, if that's the direction, you need to understand that the alternative direction has these advantages and disadvantages and the one you're leaning toward has this advantage and disadvantage.[91]

Deputy National Security Advisor J.D. Crouch concurs: 'One of the things I learned with him was never bring the cake in fully baked. As a manager, he was a guy who liked to have cookie dough on his hands.'[92] As Rumsfeld himself wrote in a memorandum entitled simply 'Assumptions':

I am often briefed by folks who begin without addressing, or seemingly having considered, understood, let alone explained, the assumptions they have made which underlie their briefing, their conclusions and their recommendations. It is a truth that you can proceed from outdated or inappropriate assumptions, perfectly logically to outdated and inappropriate conclusions. Staff folks need to be trained to develop and state assumptions at the outset of a briefing so that those being briefed know first that there are assumptions and what they are. I think that, generally, 25 to 50 percent of a briefing should be on the assumptions. If we get the assumptions right, the strategy, tactics and details follow logically.[93]

Daniel P. Fata, who worked for Rumsfeld as a deputy assistant secretary of defence, found him 'very deliberative. Rumsfeld is one of the smartest people I've ever met. His mind is always working and he thinks both conventionally, and then outside of the box.'[94]

History manager

Rumsfeld believed, given the nuance and contingency inherent in life, that one's influence over the future was limited. 'The only thing surprising,' he would remark, 'is that we continue to be surprised when a surprise occurs.'[95] The reactive core of Rumsfeld's worldview was manifested in his most famous quote, one that gave his memoir, *Known and Unknown*, its title. Rumsfeld's disquisition on the nature of knowledge revealed an underlying philosophy. A journalist suggested to the secretary that there was 'no evidence' that Saddam Hussein was working with terrorists and would consider giving them access to weapons of mass destruction:

Reports that say that something hasn't happened are always interesting to me, because as we know, there are known knowns; there are things we know we know. We also know there are known unknowns; that is to say we know there are some things we do not know. But there are also unknown unknowns -- the ones we don't know we don't know. And if one looks throughout the history of our country and other free countries, it is the latter category that tends to be the difficult one. And so people who have the omniscience that they can say with high certainty that something has not happened or is not being tried, have capabilities that are ... they can do things that I can't do.[96]

Douglas Feith argues that the key element of Rumsfeld's worldview is 'the limits of future knowledge'. Rumsfeld is 'death to predictions. His big strategic theme is uncertainty, the need to deal strategically with uncertainty. The inability to predict the future. The limits on our knowledge and limits on our intelligence.'[97] Feith wrote in his memoir that 'Rumsfeld rejected assumptions that were in the form of precise predictions. As a philosophical conservative, he considered the inevitability of error in human affairs as one of the key realities of this world.'[98] Daniel Fata said that one of Rumsfeld's recurrent questions was 'What are the unintended consequences that we aren't thinking about?'[99] This is the classic question a conservative asks when contemplating major government action.

One of his earliest memoranda during his second stint as secretary of defence laid down a basic principle for United States military action: 'When the US commits force, the task should be achievable at acceptable risk. It must be something the US is capable of accomplishing. We need to understand our limitations. The record is clear; there are some things the US simply cannot accomplish.'[100]

This could be perceived as an infuriating discursiveness or a wish to not be pinned down. But Rumsfeld was consistent in the philosophy. Consider Rumsfeld's response to a journalist who asked him about the Iraqi people's attitude toward their future. This sort of question posed to George W. Bush would invariably be met with definitive statements about the universal appeal of freedom. Rumsfeld said he didn't know what the Iraqi people thought. Challenged by the journalist about what seemed a slightly blasé answer, Rumsfeld simply noted: 'I didn't say it wasn't important to know. I said it wasn't knowable.'[101]

Director or delegator?

Rumsfeld represents a paradox on the question of assertiveness. He often maintained strong control over decision processes. This was not, as commonly portrayed, a type of megalomania, but a deep-seated preoccupation with orderliness and rigour. He disliked sloppiness, thought it harmful, and considered the imposition of rigorous analysis and proper process to be a central duty of a senior executive.

On other occasions, Rumsfeld would seek to avoid being associated with a particular decision or expressing strong views, giving subordinates tremendous latitude. In part, this was due to his complex worldview and belief that one is often managing rather than making history. Others perceived a less laudable motive. Rumsfeld's long-time friend, Steve Herbits, eventually became frustrated with what he characterized as the secretary's 'rubber glove' approach to decision making: an aversion to leaving his fingerprints behind.[102] Paul Gebhard, a special assistant to Rumsfeld, concurs that '[o]n decisions he was very wary. He didn't want people to box him in. He didn't want the fingerprints.'[103] His long-time secretary, Delonie Henry, was told by Rumsfeld to stop using a stamp embossed 'SecDef has seen' on documents coming through Rumsfeld's office. 'Just because something has come into my office and touched my inbox and gone into my outbox,' Rumsfeld told her, 'it doesn't mean I saw it, it doesn't mean I processed it....it means it moved from one box to the other, and that's all anybody will ever know for sure.' Henry detected the same 'rubber glove syndrome' as Herbits and Gebhard: 'Even though he likes to think he bellied up to the bar and took responsibility for things, if you listen and read very carefully what he said, he had a way of passing the buck.'[104]

Rumsfeld disliked inefficiency, and collected extensive data on organizational processes in order to track workflow. His memoir notes that 'over one three-month period in 2003, there were thirty-one meetings at the White House scheduled by the NSC staff. We did not receive any papers in advance for these meetings. Further, 48 percent of the meetings were cancelled and we received summaries of the conclusions for only 17 percent of the meetings held.'[105] This exercised Rumsfeld to such an extent that he wrote Condoleezza Rice repeatedly on the subject, and had an aide track these metrics for signs of improvement.[106]

His view was that the US government in national security issues had a defined chain of command. The president was in charge, while the secretary of defence was chief advisor, chief implementer, and dealt directly with regional combatant commanders.[107] He believed other positions and institutions, such as the Joint Chiefs of Staff, the White House chief of staff, and the national security advisor and staff represented unhelpful subversions of the proper order of things. Consider the commonality in Rumsfeld's complaints:

To Joint Chiefs of Staff Chairman Hugh Shelton, concerning notification of enforcement actions on Iraqi no-fly zone:[108]

- 'I'm the secretary of defense! I'm in the chain of command.'
- 'How come the combatant commanders talk to you, when they work for me?'
- 'You are not providing added value.'

To White House Chief of Staff Andy Card, concerning sending federal troops to New Orleans to help with relief operations following Hurricane Katrina:[109]

- 'Look at the chain of command. Where's the chief of staff? I report to the president. I don't report to the chief of staff. If the president really wants me to do this, he'll tell me.'

To National Security Advisor Condoleezza Rice, regarding operations of the National Security Council.

- 'Because I have failed to get you and the NSC staff to stop giving tasks and guidance to combatant commanders and the joint staff, I have drafted the attached memorandum. I had hoped it would not be necessary for me to do it this way, but since your last memo stated that we should work it out from our end, I am forced to do so. You are making a mistake. You and the NSC staff need to understand that you are not in the chain of command. Since you cannot seem to accept that fact, my only choices are to go to the president and ask him to tell you to stop or to tell anyone in DoD not to respond to you or the NSC staff. I have decided to take the latter course. If it fails, I'll have to go to the president. One way or the other, it will stop, while I am secretary of defense.'[110]

Interpersonal style
Rumsfeld's style was to thoroughly, even aggressively, interrogate those around him on basic principles, assumptions and use of language. The goal was to ensure that rigour was applied to all products coming out of the Pentagon. He disliked assertions that could not be backed up with data, and stripped down to fundamental premises. He did not impose answers, but he did ask a lot of blunt questions. As he put it to Bob Woodward, 'I tend to ask a lot of questions of the people I work with

and I tend to give very few orders. This place is so big and complicated and there's so much that I don't know, that I probe and probe and probe and push and ask, well why wasn't this done or shouldn't this be done, but it's generally with a question mark at the end.'[111]

Douglas Feith characterized the process: 'Rumsfeld worked on strategic analysis through a kind of Socratic method of question and answer. He had a way of getting people to offer him back his own ideas, as if they were their own. It was a tour de force of reason and education, not compulsion. But it could be discomforting for those on the receiving end.'[112] A senior administration official said that Rumsfeld was 'a kind of typical lightweight wrestler. His management style is always to be in your face, raising questions, playing for the advantage and to take someone down.'[113]

The proper way to work with Rumsfeld was to answer his questions, to regard them as spurs to further thinking, and to engage with the probing rather than crumble before it. Lawrence Di Rita confirms:

> He really, really liked it when people pushed back. He got a little twinkle in his eye when he saw that he had somebody who was willing to get into it. It's not really the way the Pentagon works, though senior military officers are more used to it, but you get too far detached from that and it's something that people are less inclined to do. So he sometimes had to force the discussion to come to a consensus. He rarely said 'I hereby command the following.' He knew the problems were too big, he didn't know enough to do that. He was very happy and comfortable making decisions if it was a process that was sufficiently expansive, and it was clear that there was a decision that could clearly be made.[114]

Eliot Cohen confirmed that 'He was gruff, and he was aggressive, but if you pushed back with data, you were okay. He respected that. But if you just kind of crumpled up, he was pretty relentless.'[115]

His interpersonal style was not regarded as helpful by everyone. Philip Zelikow, Counsellor at the State Department from 2005–2007, said:

> Rumsfeld appeared to draw from the commissar school of management, leading with a pistol from the back, because he would tell folks to advance, not offering his own vision of where to go, instead waiting to watch their choices and then questioning or potentially penalizing them. The style can be praised as one of delegation and prodding, but it is also designed to allow the chief to keep his own preferences obscure as long as possible.[116]

Rumsfeld's concern with precision, and desire to engage in consideration of fundamentals, led to a preference for written rather than verbal communications. He could be querulous about seemingly minor issues of vocabulary and terminology, but this was not petty pedantism. Di Rita noticed:

> Rumsfeld placed a high value in the discipline of written communication. He was very careful with language. He felt that the process of government is one that is improved through written communication. So he spent a lot of time on his own written

communications with the president and others, he insisted upon written presentations at the NSC level and at the sub-levels. So that's why you end up having a lot of documents out there from Feith and others – because that's the way he preferred to operate. He thought it disciplined your thinking, it gave people a chance to shape your thinking through written correspondence. A lot of people accuse Rumsfeld of being this clever bureaucratic infighter, but what he is is someone who is very direct about what he thinks should be happening, and he tends to commit it to writing, and people find it somehow devious. My impression was that, when it comes to government decision-making, he doesn't put a lot of stock in private oral communications between two people, because I think he recognizes that that's not the best way for a large organization to function.[117]

Memoranda from Rumsfeld's tenure reflect this work style. Some advice to Condoleezza Rice on the NSC paper flow was essentially pedagogical. For example, on the characteristics of written documents, Rumsfeld wrote that

'Papers -- Should be Easy to Read:

Papers for PCs should, as a rule, be two or three pages, i.e.:
- - Bulletized (as a rule, no more than two sentences per bullet).
- - Thoughtfully formatted (i.e., readable font, sufficient white space so notes can be made).
- - Well-edited - few, if any, 63-word sentences.

Papers should:

- - Let the reader know up front what the issue is.
- - Set out the basic facts and concepts.
- - Specify agency positions, highlighting differences.
- - Provide pros and cons for the options.'[118]

Again, whilst this could seem like pedantism, if not actively demeaning, to those in receipt of the advice, Rumsfeld viewed precise written expression as a part of thinking. As he wrote in his memoir, 'I find that committing a point of view to paper sharpens my thinking. It also permits other participants in the discussion on a given issue to understand my perspective more precisely.'[119]

As journalist Thomas Ricks put it:

It really struck me looking at some of his internal memos that he would have been a great high school English teacher. There's a muscularity and clarity and simplicity to his prose which is really unusual, not only in the US government but anywhere in American life these days. He is a good writer, and good writing, as [George] Orwell tells us, reflects good thinking.[120]

President Bush, of course, was an oral information processor and decision maker, often giving greater weight to the impression created by an interlocutor than the specific content of the conversation or written product.

The national security process in the Bush Administration

Before analyzing the Iraq decisions, we should set these two individuals in the context of the wider national security process within the Bush administration. I address the overall nature of the process, the role of the national security advisor, and the justification for focusing on the Bush/Rumsfeld dyad as the core analytical point of leverage.

By training and instinct, Bush preferred a formalistic policymaking system. He did not want to be involved in the details of policy formulation, disliked conflict amongst advisors, and prized the kind of ordered process that he had studied in the business world, with the major decisions reserved for the chief executive and loyal, talented subordinates generating options and later implementing decisions. However, he faced several difficulties in implementing this system. First, he simply did not enforce his wishes, delegating so much that he did not preserve the smooth functioning of the system. A key element of this was that he did not give sufficient backing to his national security advisor during his first term, Condoleezza Rice, to enable her to enforce his procedural and substantive wishes in the presence of powerful individuals who sought to ignore her. He was not conscious of how his behaviour impacted the system he had created. Asking for consensus recommendations in the context of deep differences over policy often led to fudged policy supported by no one. In the case of Bremer and the CPA, as we will see, he unwittingly allowed Bremer several possible reporting channels, and set up essentially a competitive system on core elements of post-war policy with Bremer, Rumsfeld and Rice all having overlapping assignments in deciding on what should happen.

Second, Donald Rumsfeld thought and operated so differently than the president that cohesive policymaking was rendered extremely difficult. A collegial approach, with a heavily engaged president drawing Rumsfeld out in debate and discussion whilst also receiving multiple other lines of information and perspective, would have illuminated, for an inquisitive executive, core points of difference between the president and the secretary of defence. As I show in the rest of the book, this did not happen.

It is important also to consider the role of the national security advisor. Coordination of national security decision making is accomplished by the National Security Council (NSC), under the direction of the national security advisor and with the support of the NSC staff. Created in 1947, the National Security Council is designed to help coordination among the national security agencies (facilitating the 'interagency process'), to provide a venue for structured debate and the generation of options, to ensure that decisions are recorded and implemented, and to provide help for the president in ensuring that decision making is orderly, thorough, and coherent.[121] Proper operation of this process could have gone a long way toward mitigating the difficulties caused by the incompatible worldviews and styles of Bush and Rumsfeld.

However, in the Bush first term, Condoleezza Rice encountered difficulties in managing this process and ensuring that principals – Rumsfeld in particular – channelled policy through it. Indeed, given the president's lack of foreign policy experience and the heavyweight nature of the principals he appointed, a managerially strong 'honest-broker' national security advisor was especially important.[122]

Whilst Rice had her weaknesses as an administrator, it is unfair to simply label her inadequate.[123] Any national security advisor faces a fundamental paradox: the role calls for the imposition of coordination and discipline on decision making, yet those who must be coordinated have more formal power and often greater experience and reputation than the supposed coordinator. Rice was well aware of this, writing in her memoirs:

> The national security advisor is staff – rarified staff, to be sure, but staff nonetheless. There's no doubt that sitting a few feet from the Oval Office confers influence, but it is the reflected influence of the president and must be used sparingly. The national security advisor must find a way to get the secretaries to do what the president wants them to do…You don't own troops, diplomats, or a budget. You have only your relationship with the president.[124]

Elliott Abrams, a senior National Security Council official in the first term and deputy national security advisor in the second, argues that Rice faced an incredibly difficult task in trying to coordinate a powerful vice president, strong secretary of defence, and a secretary of state who was the most popular political figure in the United States at the beginning of the administration. Rice was, objectively speaking, 'not of their stature', and had relatively few available means of resolving these problems:

> Was she going to deal with that problem by asserting dominance over them? Precisely how would that take place? By getting into fights every day that the president would then have to referee? Is that a smart tactic for a bureaucrat? I think she was dealing with a very difficult situation, and the president clearly did not wish to resolve it.[125]

Others have a less charitable view. Richard Perle, who served as an advisor to Rumsfeld during the first Bush term, believes that Rice fundamentally misunderstood the role of the national security advisor and the statutory process, believing that its job was to present the president with a consensus, rather than with clearly delineated options for decision. 'I served in an administration [as Assistant Secretary of Defence under Ronald Reagan]', Perle told me,

> Where options papers went to the president, and they came back with a box ticked, and with marginal notes and so forth, and one day this will all be open to historians. Reagan got significantly involved in these decisions. My impression is that Bush was much less

involved in decisions, and that the NSC under Condi regarded its task as beating a consensus out of the bureaucracy, at which point it was no longer necessary to put things before the president in a serious way.[126]

Douglas Feith also felt that Rice aimed for a consensus that too often was false, rather than presenting competing options to the president:

> Rice was unable to achieve the kind of result she preferred: to resolve interagency disputes at the level of the Principals Committee. Rather than pass along to the president a disagreement in all its naked disharmony, Rice often crafted what she called a 'bridging proposal'... [She did this] even though when Bush was presented with a clear choice among rival views, he showed the ready decisiveness of a confident executive.[127]

Lawrence Wilkerson, former chief of staff to Colin Powell and perhaps the most vociferous critic of first-term national security decision making, believes that Rice simply 'had her eye on the prize – she wanted to be secretary of state'. She did not wish to engage in battles with the other principals.[128]

The national security process, then, did not enhance the effectiveness of policymaking given the specific styles of Bush and Rumsfeld. The president was best suited to a formalistic system but did not act to preserve its operation. Bush enjoyed making fundamental decisions but not delving into the detail behind them. He would have benefited from a strong national security advisor who could challenge him to think again, and probe the assumptions and thinking of principals on his behalf.[129] It would have been especially helpful if Condoleezza Rice had been able to spell out for the president just how differently his secretary of defence thought about the key issues in Iraq, and insist that Bush confront this divergence in policy prior to late 2006.

Yet the president did not seem to want her to play this role. He would act in ways that unintentionally undermined her, or would simply ask that she sort problems out without his involvement. Bush, as reported above, did not like disagreement and did not want to be involved in policy detail. Franklin Miller of the National Security Council said:

> President Bush was not inclined to see Dr. Rice as the leader in the interagency. President Bush wanted Dr. Rice first and foremost to be his personal adviser. And so you had the makings of a bad situation, because President Bush would make decisions, but would not require agencies to carry them out. So there is no question but that the system can work, but it requires a president who is engaged, and who is prepared to push the agencies to do what he says.[130]

Rice herself recalls a revealing episode wherein she had been pushing for military planners to consider issues of 'rear-area security' in the invasion plan for Iraq. In return, she received 'uninformative slides and a rather dismissive handling of the question'. Exacerbated, she arranged a briefing with the president.

He started the meeting in a way that completely destroyed any chance of getting an answer. 'This is something Condi has wanted to talk about,' he said. I could immediately see that the generals no longer thought it to be a serious question. That is the weakness of the national security advisor's position: Authority comes from the president. If he wasn't interested in this issue, why should they care? Steve Hadley followed me to my office after the disastrous meeting. 'I would have resigned after that comment by the president,' he said.[131]

Yet Rice never forced Bush to act in ways that strengthened her position to the point where she could effectively manage the process.

This discussion of Rice – as well as the later consideration of other prominent individuals such as L. Paul Bremer and General George Casey – may raise for some readers the question of whether the predominant focus on Bush and Rumsfeld is justified. The president, of course, is the Commander in Chief and so must obviously be central to any consideration of policymaking. Why select Rumsfeld as the second point of focus? First, the structure of national security policy making accords a prominent place to the secretary of defence. This was magnified in the war on terror era, as Rumsfeld became, in the words of State Department Counsellor Eliot Cohen, the 'Deputy Commander in Chief'.[132] Iraq, from invasion and occupation to surge, was predominantly a military-politico issue and so the president and the secretary of defence were the key officials. A core paradox addressed in this study is the disjunction between means and ends in US policy in Iraq. I build the case that this is best understood as due to the different worldviews and styles of the president, who set the goals, and the secretary of defence, who determined the means employed toward achieving them.

Second, the president explicitly designated Rumsfeld, and the Department of Defence, as the lead agency in post-war Iraq with National Security Presidential Directive (NSPD-24). Even Colin Powell, often seen as the nemesis of Rumsfeld, agreed that it was logical, given the nature of the mission and the resources required, that the Pentagon and Rumsfeld play the central role. Third, Rumsfeld was, as an empirical matter, most directly involved with the management of Iraq and the making of policy. As a rough illustration of this point, I collected the most prominent in-depth journalistic accounts of the Iraq war decisions and conducted a simple tally count of the mentions of each of the Bush administration principals.[133] Rumsfeld emerges as the most discussed individual aside from the president himself, mentioned 2.3 times for every mention of Vice President Cheney. In every book, Rumsfeld is mentioned the most times. In the president's memoirs, Rumsfeld is also mentioned the most of any principal.

Finally, whilst many excellent narratives exist which offer sequential discussions about the views of each principal on the issues, this is a book of analysis, developing a case about the nature and impact of the Bush/Rumsfeld split on Iraq policy. Not only were Bush and Rumsfeld the most prominent individuals in the policy process, they also fundamentally disagreed about what should be done. Other individuals

Table 2.1   Number of references to advisors in Iraq policymaking books

	Rumsfeld	**Cheney**	**Rice**	**Powell**
Fiasco	48	17	18	20
The Gamble	28	13	4	4
Cobra II	85	24	24	32
The Endgame	43	16	26	15
Plan of Attack	186	148	123	180
State of Denial	310	86	174	70
The War Within	102	29	88	9
The Assassin's Gate	30	25	26	15
Decision Points	18	7	16	10
TOTAL	850	365	499	355

are discussed when they become particularly central to an aspect of policy, but always within the context of how their role was shaped by and related to the central Bush/Rumsfeld axis.

A brief note on sources

In a recent policy case such as Iraq, we have to be ecumenical concerning data sources. Those histories and memoirs that exist, along with contemporaneous newspaper accounts, are obviously important and I make full use of them.

Two other sources of data are used. First, a limited opening of the archives of Secretary Rumsfeld and Under-Secretary for Policy Douglas J. Feith allows for the examination of some important documents.[134] These must be handled with care – the release is partial, and from only one agency within the broad interagency process. Rumsfeld and Feith, of course, have motive to be selective in which documents they make available. Nonetheless, carefully set in context, these archives are helpful and I have made use of them.

Additionally, I conducted interviews with dozens of participants at every stage of Iraq war decision making.[135] Conducting original interviews allowed me to go beyond the information in the existing literature, and to focus on the particular questions of interest concerning Bush and Rumsfeld's influence on policymaking.

The chapters that follow represent a disaggregation of the Iraq war into significant policymaking episodes. The chapters are structured around a focused comparison of Bush and Rumsfeld's approach to each key decision, and how the interaction of these approaches shaped policy. We begin with the approach of the president and the secretary of defence to the September 11th 2001 terrorist attacks and the wider war on terror that followed.

Notes

1 Alexander L. George and Andrew Bennett, *Case Studies and Theory Development in the Social Sciences* (Cambridge, MA: MIT Press, 2005), 132–149; Stephen G. Walker and Jerrold M. Post, 'The Search for Causal Mechanisms', in *The Psychological Assessment of Political Leaders* (Ann Arbor, MI: University of Michigan Press, 2005), 63–69.

2 Richard C. Snyder, H.W. Bruck, and Burton Sapin, *Foreign Policy Decision Making: An Approach to the Study of International Relations* (New York: Free Press, 1962).

3 Kenneth N. Waltz, *Theory of International Politics* (New York: Random House, 1979).

4 Robert Jervis describes this as the 'room on fire' scenario – individual variation is overwhelmed by a situational imperative, and everyone runs for the exit. How much of international politics is captured by the 'room on fire' metaphor is a point of disagreement between those who think leaders are often important and those who think they rarely are. See Robert Jervis, *Perception and Misperception in International Politics* (Princeton, NJ: Princeton University Press, 1976), 19–21.

5 Daniel L. Byman and Kenneth N. Pollack, 'Let Us Now Praise Great Men: Bringing the Statesman Back In', *International Security* 25 (2001): 134–135.

6 Elizabeth N. Saunders, *Leaders at War: How Presidents Shape Military Interventions* (Ithaca, NY: Cornell University Press, 2011), 2–4.

7 These questions, and the concepts of 'action indispensability' and 'actor indispensability', are drawn from Fred I. Greenstein, *Personality and Politics: Problems of Evidence, Inference, and Conceptualization* (Chicago, IL: Markham, 1969).

8 See David G. Coleman, *The Fourteenth Day: JFK and the Aftermath of the Cuban Missile Crisis* (New York: WW Norton, 2012).

9 Winston S. Churchill, *The Grand Alliance* (New York: Mariner Books, 1986).

10 Greenstein, *Personality and Politics*.

11 Stephen Benedict Dyson, 'Personality and Foreign Policy: Tony Blair's Iraq Decisions', *Foreign Policy Analysis* 2 (2006): 289–306.

12 See David G. Winter, 'Assessing Leader's Personalities: A Historical Survey of Academic Research Studies', in Jerrold M. Post, ed., *The Psychological Assessment of Political Leaders* (Ann Arbor, MI: University of Michigan Press, 2003), 11–38.

13 Harrold Lasswell, *Psychopathology and Politics* (Chicago, IL: University of Chicago Press, 1930).

14 Stephen Benedict Dyson, 'Origins of the Psychological Profiling of Political Leaders: The US Office of Strategic Services and Adolf Hitler', forthcoming in *Intelligence and National Security*.

15 Alexander L. George and Juliette George, *Woodrow Wilson and Colonel House: A Personality Study* (New York: John Day, 1956).

16 See Todd S. Shultz, *Handbook of Psychobiography* (New York: Oxford University Press, 2005).

17 See Yaacov Y.I. Vertzberger, *The World in their Minds: Information Processing, Cognition, and Perception in Foreign Policy Decisionmaking* (Stanford, CA: Stanford University Press, 1990).

18 Stephen G. Walker, 'The Evolution of Operational Code Analysis', *Political Psychology* 11: 403–418.

19 See P.T. Costa and R.R. McCrae, 'Set Like Plaster? Evidence for the Stability of Adult Personality', in T.F Heatherton and J. Weinberger, eds, *Can Personality Change?* (Washington, DC: APA Books, 1994), 21–40; Margaret G. Hermann, 'Explaining Foreign Policy Behavior Using the Personal Characteristics of Political Leaders', *International Studies Quarterly* 24: 7–46.

20 Mark Schafer, 'Issues in Assessing Psychological Characteristics at a Distance', *Political Psychology*, 21 (2000): 511–527.

21 Stephen Benedict Dyson, 'Cognitive Style and Foreign Policy: Margaret Thatcher's Black-and-White Thinking', *International Political Science Review*, 30 (2009): 33–49; Peter Suedfeld. 'The Complexity Construct in Political Psychology: Personological and Cognitive Approaches'. 2010. Available at www.pubs.drdc.gc.ca/…/CEBsupport.100218_0834. Toronto_CR_2010_022.pdf; Peter Suedfeld and Philip Tetlock, 'Integrative Complexity of Communication in International Crises', *Journal of Conflict Resolution* 21 (1977): 169–184.

22 Betty Glad, 'Black-and-white thinking: Ronald Reagan's approach to foreign policy', *Political Psychology*, 4, 1, 1983, pp. 33–76.

23 E.J. Dionne, 'Who is Obama? Now We Know', *Washington Post*, 4 May 2011, www.washingtonpost.com/opinions/obama-the-bold-now-we-know/2011/05/04/AFmmUorF_story.html.

24 Margaret G. Hermann, 'Assessing Leadership Style: Trait Analysis', in Jerrold M. Post, ed., *The Psychological Assessment of Political Leaders* (Ann Arbor, MI, University of Michigan Press, 2003): 195–196.

25 See Henry A. Kissinger, *A World Restored: Metternich, Castlereagh and the Problems of Peace, 1812–1822* (New York: Mariner Books, 1973); Robert A. Kaplan, 'Kissinger, Metternich, and Realism', *The Atlantic*, June 1999, available at www.theatlantic.com/past/docs/issues/99jun/9906kissinger.htm.

26 Alexander L. George, 'The Operational Code: A Neglected Approach to the Study of Political Leaders and Decision Making', *International Studies Quarterly*, 1969: 190–222.

27 See Thomas Carlyle, 'The Leader as Hero', and Herbert Spencer, 'The Great Man Theory Breaks Down', both in Barbara Kellerman, ed., *Political Leadership: A Source Book* (Pittsburgh, PA: University of Pittsburgh Press, 1986): 5–9 and 10–15.

28 Hermann, 'Assessing Leadership Style', 188–190; Sidney Hook, 'The Eventful Man and the Event-Making Man', in Kellerman, ed., *Political Leadership*, 24–35.

29 Thomas Blanton, 'US Policy and the Revolutions of 1989', in Svetlana Savranskaya, Thomas Blanton and Vladislav Zubok, eds, *'Masterpieces of History': The Peaceful End of the Cold War in Europe, 1989* (Budapest/New York: Central European University Press, 2010).

30 For a similar argument on the important of studying both external and internal element of style ('purpose' and 'process' in Hargrove's words), see Erwin C. Hargrove, 'Presidential Personality and Leadership Style', in *Researching the Presidency: Vital Questions, New Approaches*, George C. Edwards III, John H. Kessel, and Bert A. Rockman, eds (Pittsburgh, PA: University of Pittsburgh Press, 1993) 69–110.

31 Richard Tanner Johnson, *Managing the White House: An Intimate Study of the Presidency* (New York: Harper & Row, 1974); see also John P. Burke, *The Institutional Presidency* (Baltimore, MD: Johns Hopkins University Press, 1992), 58–89; Stephen Hess, *Organizing the Presidency* (Washington, DC: The Brookings Institution, 1976); Roger B. Porter, *Presidential Decision Making* (New York: Cambridge University Press, 1980).

32 Johnson, *Managing the White House*, 9–38.

33 Johnson, *Managing the White House*, 74–119, 199–229.

34 Johnson, *Managing the White House*, 120–158.

35 Karen M. Hult, 'Advising the President', in George C. Edwards III, John H. Kessel and Bert A. Rockman, eds, *Researching the Presidency: Vital Questions, New Approaches* (Pittsburgh, PA: University of Pittsburgh Press, 1993), 114.

36 Patrick J. Haney, *Organizing for Foreign Policy Crises: Presidents, Advisers, and the Management of Decision Making* (Ann Arbor, MI: University of Michigan Press, 1997).

37   Meena Bose, *Shaping and Signaling Presidential Policy: The National Security Decision Making of Eisenhower and Kennedy* (College Station, TX: Texas A&M University Press, 1998), 99.

38   Bert A. Rockman, 'Staffing and Organizing the Presidency', in Robert Y. Shapiro, Martha Joynt Kumar, and Lawrence R. Jacobs, eds, *Presidential Power: Forging the Presidency for the Twenty-First Century* (New York: Columbia University Press, 2000), 169–171.

39   Alexander L. George, *Presidential Decisionmaking in Foreign Policy: The Effective Use of Information and Advice* (Boulder, CO: Westview Press, 1980), 147. See also Richard W. Cottam and Bert Rockman, 'In the Shadow of Substance: Presidents as Foreign Policy Makers'. In David P. Forsythe, ed., *American Foreign Policy in an Uncertain World* (Lincoln, NE: University of Nebraska Press, 1984).

40   Bose, *Shaping and Signaling Presidential Policy*, 110.

41   Quoted in Rothkopf, *Running the World*, 409.

42   Johnson, *Managing the White House*, 178.

43   David J. Rothkopf, *Running the World: The Inside Story of the National Security Council and the Architects of American Power* (New York: Public Affairs, 2005), 14.

44   Cecil B. Crabb, Jr and Kevin V. Mulcahy, *Presidents and Foreign Policy Making: From FDR to Reagan* (Baton Rouge, LA: Louisiana State University Press, 1986); Thomas Preston, *The President and his Inner Circle* (New York: Columbia University Press, 2001). Thomas Preston and Paul t'Hart, 'Understanding and Evaluating Bureaucratic Politics: The Nexus Between Political Leaders and Advisory Systems', *Political Psychology* 20 (1999): 49–98.

45   Alexander L. George and Eric Stern, 'Presidential Management Styles and Models', in Alexander L. George and Juliette George, *Presidential Personality and Performance* (Boulder, CO: Westview Press, 1998): 222–234.

46   Erwin C. Hargrove, *Jimmy Carter as President: Leadership and the Politics of the Public Good* (Baton Rouge, LA: Louisiana State University Press, 1988).

47   George, *Presidential Decisionmaking*, 148.

48   Johnson, *Managing the White House*.

49   Steven Rattner, *Overhaul: An Insider's Account of the Obama Administration's Emergency Rescue of the Auto Industry* (New York: Houghton Mifflin, 2010), 133.

50   Quoted in Peter Rodman, *Presidential Command: Power, Leadership, and the Making of Foreign Policy from Richard Nixon to George W. Bush* (New York: Alfred A. Knopf, 2009) 232.

51   See Robert Draper, *Dead Certain* (New York: The Free Press, 2007), 88, 106, 291, and passim; Bob Woodward, *State of Denial* (New York: Simon & Schuster, 2006), passim; Evan Thomas and Richard Wolffe, 'Bush in the Bubble', *Newsweek*, 19 December 2005, 29–39; Ron Suskind, 'Without a Doubt', *New York Times Magazine*, 17 October 2004; Scott McClellan, *What Happened* (New York: Public Affairs, 2008), 128, 145, 208; Bill Keller, 'The Radical Presidency of George W. Bush: Reagan's Son', *New York Times Magazine*, 26 January 2003; Mike Allen, 'Close Look at a Focused President', *Washington Post*, 27 April 2003, A04; Fred I. Greenstein, 'The Leadership Style of George W. Bush', in Fred I. Greenstein, ed., *The George W. Bush Presidency: An Early Assessment* (Baltimore, MD: Johns Hopkins University Press, 2004) 1–17.

52   As told to Bob Woodward, *Bush at War*, 136–137.

53   George W. Bush, *Decision Points* (New York: Broadway, 2011), 140.

54   Stephen Benedict Dyson, *The Blair Identity: Leadership and Foreign Policy* (Manchester: Manchester University Press, 2009).

55   Tony Blair, *A Journey: My Political Life* (New York: Alfred A. Knopf, 2010), 393.

56   Draper, *Dead Certain*, x.

57   McClellan, *What Happened*, 208.

58 Cullen Murphy and Todd S. Purdum, 'Fairwell to All That: An Oral History of the Bush Whitehouse', *Vanity Fair*, February 2009. www.vanityfair.com/politics/features/2009/02/bush-oral-history200902.

59 See Draper, *Dead Certain*, xv, 357, and passim; McClellan, *What Happened*, 207; Fred Barnes, *Rebel in Chief* (New York: Three Rivers Press, 2006), 21–24, 86–87, 110–111, 200.

60 Dick Kirschten, 'Bush as Boss: The Leadership Style of the Man Who Could be Government's Next CEO', *Government Executive*, July 2000, www.govexec.com/features/0700/0700s1.htm.

61 Draper, *Dead Certain*, 352.

62 Author Interview with Peter Feaver, Boston, MA, 28 August 2008.

63 Draper, *Dead Certain*, 15.

64 Richard Brookhiser, 'Close Up: The Mind of George W. Bush', *The Atlantic Monthly*, April 2003, www.theatlantic.com/past/docs/issues/2003/04/brookhiser.htm.

65 Rothkopf, *Running the World*, 397.

66 See Barnes, *Rebel in Chief*, 44, 95, 104, 208; Keller, 'The Radical Presidency'.

67 David Frum, *The Right Man* (New York: Wiedenfeld & Nicholson, 2003), 276.

68 Joshua Muravchik, 'Two Cheers: Second Thoughts on the Bush Doctrine', *World Affairs Journal* (autumn 2008): 57–70.

69 Author interview with Peter Wehner, by telephone, 16 October 2008.

70 Keller, 'The Radical Presidency'.

71 Draper, *Dead Certain*, 11.

72 Draper, *Dead Certain*, 357.

73 Richard Baehr with Thomas Lifson, 'GWB: HBS, MBA', *American Thinker*, 3 February 2004, www.americanthinker.com/printpage/?url=http://www.americanthinker.com/archived-articles/../2004/02/gwb_hbs_mba.html.

74 Bush, *Decision Points*, 22.

75 Rodman, *Presidential Command*, 235.

76 Draper, *Dead Certain*, 46.

77 Author interview with Lawrence Wilkerson, 23 January 2009, Washington, DC.

78 Author interview with Franklin C. Miller, 6 August 2009, Washington, DC.

79 Donald H. Rumsfeld, *Known and Unknown* (New York: Sentinel, 2011), 319.

80 Rodman, *Presidential Command*, 235.

81 Woodward, *Bush at War*, 259.

82 Byron J. York, 'Bush Loyalty Test', *National Review Online*, 30 December 2008, www.nationalreview.com/articles/226613/bush-loyalty-test/byron-york.

83 Author interview with Eliot Cohen, 19 February 2009, Washington, DC.

84 Douglas Feith, *War and Decision*, 212.

85 Eric Schmitt and Thom Shanker, *Counterstrike: The Untold Story of America's Secret Campaign Against Al Qaeda* (New York: St. Martin's Press, 2012), 53.

86 Author interview with Lawrence Di Rita.

87 Rumsfeld, *Known and Unknown*, 667.

88 *PBS Frontline*, Interview with Thomas White. Available at www.pbs.org/wgbh/pages/frontline/shows/pentagon/interviews/white.html.

89 Quoted in James Fallows, *Blind Into Baghdad: America's War in Iraq* (New York: Vintage, 2006), 45.

90 Graham, *By His Own Rules*, 552.

91 Woodward, *Plan of Attack*, 181.

92 Graham, *By His Own Rules*, 527.

93   Donald H. Rumsfeld, 'Assumptions', 18 October 2002, http://library.Rumsfeld.com/doclib/sp/296/Re%20Assumptions%2010-18-2002.pdf.

94   Author interview with Daniel P. Fata, 24 November 2009, Washington, DC.

95   Rumsfeld, *Known and Unknown*, 334.

96   Department of Defense News Briefing, Secretary Rumsfeld and General Myers, 12 February 2002, www.defense.gov/transcripts/transcript.aspx?transcriptid=2636.

97   Fallows, *Blind into Baghdad*, 45.

98   Feith, *War and Decision*, 110.

99   Author interview with Fata.

100 Rumsfeld, 'Guidelines When Considering Committing US Forces', March 2001, http://library.Rumsfeld.com/doclib/sp/311/2001-03%20Guidelines%20When%20Considering%20Committing%20US%20Forces%20(II-93-5).pdf.

101 Todd S. Purdum, 'Rumsfeld's Imperious Style Turns Combative', *New York Times*, 30 March 2003, 10.

102 Woodward, *State of Denial*, 317.

103 Graham, *By His Own Rules*, 681.

104 Graham, *By His Own Rules*, 518.

105 Rumsfeld, *Known and Unknown*, 328.

106 Lieutenant General Bantz Craddock to Rumsfeld, 'PC & NSC Meetings: Are We Improving?' 29 May 2004. http://library.Rumsfeld.com/doclib/sp/258/From%20LTG%20Craddock%20re%20PC%20and%20NSC%20Meetings-%20Are%20We%20Improving%2005-29-2004.pdf#search="PC NSC Meetings".

107 Graham, *By His Own Rules*, 515.

108 Woodward, *State of Denial*, 18, 34, 38.

109 Graham, *By His Own Rules*, 515.

110 Donald Rumsfeld to Condoleezza Rice, 'Chain of Command', 2 December 2002, http://library.Rumsfeld.com/doclib/sp/242/To%20Condoleezza%20Rice%20re%20Chain%20of%20Command%2012-02-2002.pdf.

111 Woodward, *Plan of Attack*, 43.

112 Feith cited in Graham, *By His Own Rules*, 327. See also Thom Shanker and Eric Schmitt, 'Rumsfeld Seeks Consensus Through Jousting', *New York Times*, 19 March 2003, 1.

113 Elisabeth Bumiller and Eric Schmitt, 'On the Job and at Home, Influential Hawks' 30-year Friendship Evolves', *New York Times*, 11 September 2002, 20.

114 Author interview with Lawrence Di Rita.

115 Author interview with Eliot Cohen.

116 Thomas Ricks, *The Gamble* (New York: Penguin, 2009).

117 Author interview with Di Rita.

118 Donald Rumsfeld to Condoleezza Rice, 'Interagency Process', 8 August 2002, http://library.Rumsfeld.com/doclib/sp/243/To%20Condoleezza%20Rice%20re%20Interagency%20Process%2008-20-2002.pdf#search="interagency process".

119 Rumsfeld, *Known and Unknown*, 324.

120 *PBS Frontline*, Interview with Thomas Ricks. Available at www.pbs.org/wgbh/pages/frontline/shows/pentagon/interviews/ricks.html.

121 David Rothkopf, *Running the World: The Inside Story of the National Security Council and the Architects of American Power* (New York: Public Affairs, 2005); Ivo H. Daalder and I.M. Destler, *In the Shadow of the Oval Office: Profiles of the National Security Advisers and the Presidents They Served* (New York: Simon & Schuster, 2009); John P. Burke, *Honest Broker? The National Security Advisor and Presidential Decision Making* (College Station, TX: Texas A&M University Press, 2009).

122 Burke, *Honest Broker*, 239.
123 See John Burke, 'Condoleezza Rice as NSC Advisor: A Case Study of the Honest Broker Role', *Presidential Studies Quarterly* 35 (2005) 554–575.
124 Condoleezza Rice, *No Higher Honor: A Memoir of my Years in Washington* (New York: Crown, 2011), 11.
125 Author interview with Elliott Abrams, Washington, DC, 11 March 2009.
126 Author interview with Richard Perle, by telephone, 14 January 2009.
127 Douglas Feith, *War and Decision: Inside the Pentagon at the Dawn of the War on Terror* (New York: Harper, 2008), 143–144.
128 Author interview with Lawrence Wilkerson, Washington, DC, 23 January 2009.
129 James P. Pfiffner, 'Policy Making in the Bush White House', *Issues in Governance Studies* 21 (2008), 8.
130 Author interview with Franklin C. Miller, Washington, DC, 6 August 2009.
131 Rice, *No Higher Honor*, 189–190.
132 C-SPAN, 'Q & A With Eliot Cohen' 25 June 2005.
133 Thomas E. Ricks, *Fiasco* and *The Gamble* (New York: Penguin, 2006; 2009); Michael R. Gordon and Bernard E. Trainor, *Cobra II; The Endgame* (New York: Pantheon, 2006; 2012) Bob Woodward, *Plan of Attack; State of Denial; The War Within* (New York: Simon & Schuster, 2004; 2006; 2008); George Packer, *The Assassin's Gate* (New York: Farrar, Straus and Giroux, 2006); George W. Bush, *Decision Points* (New York: Broadway, 2011).
134 See www.Rumsfeld.com and www.waranddecision.com.
135 Interviews were conducted with Elliott Abrams, Senior Director on the NSC and Deputy National Security Advisor for Global Democracy Strategy; Stephen D. Biddle, Senior fellow, Council on Foreign Relations, Advisor to Bush Administration, especially during 'surge' decision period; John Bolton, Ambassador to the United Nations; Eliot A. Cohen, Counselor to Secretary of State Rice; Charles A. Duelfer, UNSCOM Deputy Head, author of 'Duelfer report' on Saddam's WMD; Daniel P. Fata, Deputy Assistant Secretary of Defense; Peter D. Feaver, Senior Director, National Security Council, author of 'National Strategy for Victory in Iraq' and key architect of surge policy; Douglas J. Feith, Under Secretary of Defense for Policy. Senior Pentagon official for postwar planning; Marc Grossman, Under Secretary of State; Kim R. Holmes, Assistant Secretary of State; Edwin Meese III, Fmr Attorney General, member of Iraq Study Group; Franklin C. Miller, Senior Director for Iraq on the National Security Council; Joshua Muravchik, neoconservative scholar, originator of democracy promotion agenda; Noam Neusner, Bush speechwriter; Lt. Col (ret.) John Nagl, advisor to General David Petraeus, author of US army Counterinsurgency field manual, which was at the heart of 'surge' doctrine change; Richard Perle, member of Defense Policy Board, leading neoconservative; Lawrence Di Rita, senior advisor to Rumsfeld, later Pentagon spokesperson; Fmr Senator Chuck Robb, member of Iraq Study Group; Fmr Congressman Rob Simmons, Republican foreign policy expert; Peter Wehner, Director of Bush Administration's Office of Strategic Initiatives; Col. Lawrence Wilkerson, Chief of Staff for Secretary of State Colin Powell, and others who preferred to remain anonymous.

3

The emergence of the Bush doctrine

President Bush – who came into office with neither interest nor experience in foreign affairs – was motivated to think deeply about foreign policy by the September 11th 2001 terrorist attacks. He worked out his foreign policy beliefs in a context of fear, anger and threat. His response to the attacks was shaped by his black-and-white thinking and history-making temperament.

Bush elucidated three principles to undergird the US response.[1] First, states that harbour terrorists would be seen as equally culpable, and as subject to armed action, as terrorist groups themselves. The paramount threat was the nexus between dictatorships, states with the potential to acquire weapons of mass destruction, and terrorist groups. Second, Bush would conduct foreign policy on the front foot, preferring pre-emption to reaction. Third, the president's long-term strategy was to advance democracy, especially in the Middle East, as a means to remove the preconditions for terrorism.

These principles fit the president's temperament. Bush was inclined toward proactive policies, and clear-cut delineations of good and evil. Other individuals who could have been president in his place would have adopted a different strategic view, and United States policy would have been materially altered from the path that led to the Iraq war. Bush was in a position to shape history, and who he was shaped the choices he made.

Secretary Rumsfeld reacted to 9/11 in a very different way. His basic temperament and worldview was very different from Bush's. Rumsfeld was leery of proactive policies and costly commitments. He was suspicious of moralizing. He saw the world as more complex and less amenable to change than the president. Whilst Rumsfeld was a believer in power politics and a nationalist, and so supportive of some aspects of post-9/11 strategy, he was never comfortable with the president's commitment to the spread of democracy and the huge, long-lasting commitments that agenda implied. Where the president responded emotionally, Rumsfeld responded analytically.

The Bush doctrine, then, was very much Bush's choice. His personality and leadership style were essential in shaping the US response to the terrorist attacks. In this chapter I analyze Bush's instant responses to 9/11, as he made the fundamental decision that the US would engage in a war on terror. I then trace the development of the key principles of the Bush doctrine, and examine whether these were ideas original to the president or pre-existing views of neoconservatives in his administration. I consider other strategic responses that Bush could have chosen – realist, liberal internationalist, isolationist – and show how they were inconsistent with his temperament. I then consider Secretary Rumsfeld's response to 9/11, tracing the beginnings of the divergence in ideas between the president and the secretary of defence.

Table 3.1 gives an overview of the impact of the two leaders during the period following 9/11. The chapter traces this impact and elaborates upon these core points.

Bush's immediate reactions to 9/11

The shock of 9/11 motivated Bush to give deep thought to international affairs, in a context of fear, anger and threat.[2] Bush's temperament conditioned his experience

Table 3.1   Bush, Rumsfeld and the emergence of the Bush doctrine

Bush's traits	The Bush doctrine	Rumsfeld's traits	The Bush doctrine
Black-and-white worldview	War on terror as good vs. evil. Equivalence of terrorists and states that harbour them. Moral component – democracy agenda.	Complex worldview	Suspicious of doctrines. Disliked war on terror label. Rejected talk of good vs. evil.
History maker	Preemption – foreign policy on the front foot. Less revolutionary strategies not chosen.	History manager	Rejection of idea of imposing democracy abroad.
Delegator	States broad goals, but little in terms of specifics as to how to achieve them.	Dictator or delegator?	Reticence in directly stating alternatives to Bush doctrine. Did not express strong view on whether to invade Iraq.

of this shock. The interaction of these situational and personal elements resulted in a shift from the basically realist Bush administration foreign policy of pre-9/11 to the clear-cut, proactive moralism of the Bush doctrine.

On September 11th 2001, Bush was visiting the Emma E. Booker elementary school in Sarasota, Florida, reading to a group of 7 year olds. At 9:05am, Chief of Staff Andy Card crossed to where the president was sitting, leaned in, and whispered 'A second plane has hit the World Trade Center. America is under attack.'[3] This is the first key moment in recovering the psychological life of 9/11 as experienced by the president.[4]

'I'm very aware of the cameras,' he recalled. 'I'm trying to absorb that knowledge. I have nobody to talk to. I'm sitting in the midst of a classroom with little kids, listening to a children's story and I realize I'm the Commander in Chief and the country has just come under attack.'[5] Bush immediately reached the foundational judgement of his presidency: 'They had declared war on us, and I made up my mind at that moment that we were going to war.'[6] He later wrote 'My first reaction was outrage. Someone had dared attack America. They were going to pay.'[7]

Bush found a television and watched replaying images of the planes striking the World Trade Center. An aide recalled that Bush watched the recording twice, then 'wheeled away with this look of absolute – I guess you'd have to say disgust more than hatred – on his face.'[8] He walked out to speak to the press – national television networks breaking into normal programming to carry his words: 'Today, we have had a national tragedy. Two airplanes have crashed into the World Trade Center. We're going to hunt down those folks who committed this act. Terrorism against our nation will not stand.'[9] It was a statement based on the president's immediate reactions. This showed in the discordant colloquialism ('those folks…'), and a familiar familial phrasing: 'Terrorism against our nation will not stand,' that recalled President George H.W. Bush's reaction to Iraq's invasion of Kuwait in August 1990. Asked later how he composed the statement, Bush said 'why I came up with those specific words, maybe it was an echo from the past… I'll tell you this, we didn't sit around massaging the words. I just got up and spoke.'[10]

Bush left Florida on Air Force One. 'I guess we're at war,' he told aides at around 9.50am, the first time he had vocalized this judgement. In a call to the vice president, Bush was angry: 'Whoever did this isn't going to like having me as president';[11] 'we're going to find out who did this… and we're going to kick their asses.'[12] 'My blood was boiling,' he later wrote.[13]

The president's plane flew to Barksdale Air Force base in Shreveport, Louisiana, landing at 11.45am. Bush spoke again to Vice President Cheney, maintaining his level of outrage at the 'faceless cowards' who had attacked America and – in what would become a recurrent emphasis of the president's approach in the coming days – telling Cheney that America had to prepare for a 'new war'. Bush addressed the nation on television using much the same terms: 'Freedom itself was attacked this morning by a faceless coward, and freedom will be defended.'[14]

At 3.15pm, Bush convened the first National Security Council meeting of the new era. National Security Advisor Condoleezza Rice recalls that Bush was in incisive form: 'We are at war,' was his opening demarche. 'This is an attack on freedom, and we are going to treat it as such.'[15]

Bush reiterated these themes in a further nationwide address that evening. The attacks were 'evil, despicable acts' representing 'the worst of human nature'. He used, for the first time, the phrase 'war against terrorism'.[16] On retiring to bed, Bush wrote in his diary that 'the Pearl Harbor of the 21st Century took place today.'[17]

Much of the 'Bush doctrine' was apparent in the president's earliest reactions to 9/11. Those sentiments were woven into a cohesive strategic framework over the coming months, with the significant addition of democracy promotion as a long-term response to terrorism. The doctrine was codified in a series of speeches, and a new national security document, which punctuated the period from the September 11th 2001 terrorist attacks to the March 2003 invasion of Iraq.

Terrorists, dictators, and weapons of mass destruction

President Bush used the January 2002 State of the Union speech to continue to elaborate the principals of his new foreign policy. The president's first priority was to pursue terrorists who 'consider the entire world a battlefield'. The doctrine the president proclaimed on 9/11 of making no distinction between terrorists and states that harbour them was fully explained. Bush differentiated between two classes of harbouring states. The first were allies who were as threatened by terrorists as the US itself. These states were plagued by 'terrorist parasites', but many – such as the newly helpful Pakistan – were '*now* fighting terror', having undergone an improvement in attitude in recent months. A second class of harbouring state was identified: regimes with a fondness for sponsoring terrorism and a capacity to pursue weapons of mass destruction. These states had, Bush said, been 'pretty quiet' since 9/11, but remained dangerous. 'We know their true nature.' Three states, North Korea, Iran, and Iraq, were collected under the umbrella term, 'the Axis of Evil'.

Bush spoke at greatest length about what he considered to be the most heinous state in the axis: Iraq. North Korea's offences were allotted seventeen words. Iran's nineteen. Iraq was indicted in an eighty-four word barrage. Where North Korea and Iran had committed the vague evils of denying freedom and pursuing WMD, the charges against Iraq were more specific. The regime 'plotted to develop anthrax, nerve gas, and nuclear weapons'. Their evil was not latent and potential, but active and manifest, as the regime 'used poison gas to murder thousands of its own citizens, leaving the bodies of mothers huddled over their dead children.'[18]

Bush returned to this theme one year later in the 2003 State of the Union speech, which pointed clearly toward war with Iraq. First, the president invited the American people to understand his job since 9/11. 'There are days when our fellow citizens do not hear news about the war on terror. There is never a day when I do not learn of another threat, or receive reports of operations in progress, or give an order in this global war against a scattered network of killers.' Bush offered a more precise definition of the 'axis of evil' that is 'the gravest danger facing America': 'outlaw regimes that seek and possess nuclear, chemical, and biological weapons' and could 'give or sell these weapons to terrorist allies.' The indictment ended on the terrain that the president was most comfortable with, the clarity of moral judgement:

> The dictator who is assembling the world's most dangerous weapons has already used them on whole villages leaving thousands of his own citizens dead, blind or disfigured. Iraqi refugees tell us how forced confessions are obtained: by torturing children while their parents are made to watch. International human rights groups have catalogued other methods used in the torture chambers of Iraq: electric shock, burning with hot irons, dripping acid on the skin, mutilation with electric drills, cutting out tongues and rape. If this is not evil then evil has no meaning.[19]

The linking of terrorists, rogue states, and weapons of mass destruction placed together in one category several kinds of problem. The great benefit, at least in terms of producing a comprehensive strategic response, is that it cut through a lot of ambiguity and offered a clear diagnosis of the problem. This very simplic-ity was criticized by many, who would see the problems of terrorists, dictators and proliferation as different from one another and requiring nuanced and tailored policy responses. But to an individual with Bush's angular mind and intolerance of ambiguity, the linking of these three issues – glossed with indignation against the immoralities of terrorism and dictatorship – was appealing.

Pre-emption

The second key element of the doctrine was to embrace the principle of acting before threats were fully formed. Pre-emption was consonant with Bush's decisive nature and his history-making leadership stance.[20]

The president introduced the policy of pre-emption at the 2002 West Point Military Academy commencement ceremony. Bush believed pre-emption was necessary because of the link between terrorism, dictators and WMD. 'Even weak states [like Iraq] and small groups [like Al-Qaeda] could attain a catastrophic power to strike great nations. Our enemies have declared this very intention and have been caught seeking these terrible weapons.' In these circumstances, the Cold War-era reliance on containment would not suffice. In Bush's view, President Bill Clinton had used an updated version of that strategy with Iraq and it had been unsuccessful. What was needed was 'to take the battle to the enemy'. If nations pursuing threatening weapons were allowed to 'fully materialize' them, 'we will have waited too long'. All Americans – but one imagines these West Pointers more immediately than most – were required 'to be forward-looking and resolute, to be ready for pre-emptive action when necessary to defend our liberty and to defend our lives'. The number one target: 'unbalanced dictators with weapons of mass destruction.'[21]

Pre-emption was a replacement, then, for containment. Under a doctrine of containment, security was ensured by a strong defence. The enemy would be unable to attack either because they were boxed-in physically, in the way that the US built defences against Soviet incursion in Western Europe, or psychologically, by the threat of massive retaliation in response to aggression. Neither tactic would work against the new enemy, Bush concluded. Physical defence was problematic, as by its very nature terrorism struck at unexpected times and in unexpected places. Deterrence was difficult as terrorist groups did not have territory against which to retaliate, and it was not clear that they calculated costs and benefits in the same way as had the leadership of the modern, industrialized Soviet Union.[22]

Not everyone agreed that this analysis of the problems of containing terrorism extended to a state such as Iraq, which did have territory against which retaliation was possible.[23] The president, though, did not make this distinction, believing that a commonality of evil and a shared hatred of the United States made pre-emption equally applicable to terrorist groups and rogue dictatorships.

Moralism, religiosity, and democracy promotion

One of Bush's personal friends, commenting on his approach to post-9/11 foreign policy, said that 'I think, in his frame, this is what God has asked him to do. It offers him enormous clarity.'[24] The moralism and sense of mission Bush derived from his faith disposed him toward an agenda that was not limited to the uncompromising use of hard power and a very low tolerance of threat. A more positive expression of the president's moralism was necessary to round out the Bush doctrine: the promotion of democracy.

As Bush said to Counsellor Karen Hughes, 'This is a defining moment. We have an opportunity to restructure the world toward freedom, and we have to get it right.'[25] Absent this belief, it is possible to imagine the president shifting in a hawkish direction, but more difficult to see him adopting democracy promotion as a core goal. Indeed, there is a possibility for a crude controlled comparison here. The vice president, operating in the same circumstances, also shifted his worldview in a hawkish direction. But Cheney did not internalize the more idealist set of principles. As Victor Davis Hanson, who spent time with both President Bush and Vice President Cheney, puts it, Bush had 'a lot more propensity to be idealistic and see that democracy is the innate right of mankind…. [the US] should be the one to offer the world our values.' Cheney's view 'is much more tragic'. On Iraq, he would say 'This is a messy transition, and I don't know whether or not it's going to work, and I don't know whether people in the Middle East are capable of democracy.'[26] Like Cheney, as discussed below, Rumsfeld was unconvinced by the wisdom of a democracy promotion agenda. Recall the key question posed earlier: would another individual, in the same position after 9/11, have made the same choices? Cheney and Rumsfeld faced the same circumstances as Bush, and thought differently on the question of democracy promotion.

'Bush embraced democratization as a kind of historical and divine imperative,' writes Charles Kessler. 'The president does have a strong moral streak,' says Condoleezza Rice. 'Certain things are right. Certain things offend him. People living under tyranny offends him.'[27] Rice was herself converted to support for democracy promotion by Bush's advocacy of the approach.

Peter Wehner, the White House director of strategic initiatives, explained that '[Bush's] moral framework, which he's spoken about dozens and dozens of times, is his view of freedom. And it is a kind of teleological issue, that people are created to be free, and that leads to, many more times than not, human flourishing, and human excellence.'[28] Wehner stresses that Bush 'did not regard the Bible as a handbook to foreign policy,' and that moralism, rather than Christianity per se, is the key driver: 'the president is Christian, and I think that that has shaped his views of the human person, but a lot of the commentary that I've seen about it is terribly simplistic – his reading of the Bible led him to invade Iraq – that's preposterous. But does a certain religious view, and moral view, play a role in that? Yes.'[29]

Eliot Cohen feels that Bush had 'a core belief in the dignity of individuals and freedom as a divine gift of some kind. That's just a core belief.' Bush, Cohen stresses, was driven by the interaction of his moralistic, faith-driven temperament and the searing experience of 9/11:

> Part of the commitment to the Freedom Agenda comes about from thinking about how did we get to 9/11, and it came from the belief that simply accommodating yourself to thuggish regimes, and hoping they will keep the crazies under control, turned out to be a big mistake. You could have come to that conclusion, actually, from the Iranian revolution. You probably should have. But the reaction to 9/11 is the most important thing. And again, it will take decades until the partisan debates settle down, for people to appreciate just how searing the 9/11 experience was. And that I think is the master key to understanding what went on. The people who had to live through that, and who had the feeling that they were really responsible for the security of the United States, they faced this challenge that they hadn't really thought about a whole lot before.[30]

Bush's democracy promotion agenda would be criticized from both the political left and right as unrealistic. The lack of political purchase achieved by the Freedom Agenda strengthens the argument for its adoption being the product of dispositional, individual-level factors: the motivation was certainly not a cynical grab for popularity. Bing West read it as evidence that the president was making policy based on 'transcendental principle' rather than 'a practical strategy that matched resources to policy goals'. For West, 'eschatological faith' had supplanted reason.[31] Scott McClellan reports that Bush was equally insistent on his 'Freedom Agenda' in private and in public: 'There was nothing I would ever see him talk more passionately about than this view, both publicly and privately.'[32]

Bush became committed to the cause of pro-democracy exiles from authoritarian systems. Natan Sharansky's book *The Case for Democracy* was read closely by Bush, who commented that 'if you want a glimpse of how I think about foreign policy, read Natan Sharansky's book.'[33] Less known is that Bush regularly had groups of exiles brought to visit him in the White House. Carl Gershman, the head of the non-partisan National Endowment for Democracy, was prevailed upon to bring visiting dissidents in for private sessions with the president, who was deeply moved by these experiences.[34]

Neoconservatives and the Bush doctrine

George W. Bush was not, of course, the first person to think of the three ideas that comprised his doctrine, and it would be reductionist to seek to explain them as purely a result of his private thought. Some second and third-tier officials in his administration had been promoting ideas such as pre-emption and the terrorist / dictator nexus for several years. My argument, then, is that a specific combination of these ideas – along with a commitment to democratization – was especially appealing to the president following 9/11. As Peter Wehner puts it:

> I think there were dispositions [in the president's approach to foreign policy], and those dispositions were released and unlocked in the aftermath of 9/11. If 9/11 hadn't happened, then I think the foreign policy approach would have been quite different. There just wouldn't have been the moment, the opportunity, to try and shape things like he did.[35]

Some have suggested that we should look for the origins of the Bush doctrine not in the temperament of the president but instead in the writings and policy machinations of neoconservatives. Joshua Micah Marshall, in an influential *Foreign Affairs* article, states this thesis:

> [D]espite being relegated to the second tier of executive branch appointments and various positions in the conservative foreign policy establishment outside of the government, the neo-cons have been peculiarly capable of advancing their views with their superiors. The defining characteristic of the Bush administration's foreign policy, in fact, has been the way the neo-cons in and out of office have been able to win so many of the key battles - if not on the first go-round, then on the second or the third. The neo-cons have not always written the libretto, but the score has in most cases remained firmly in their hands, and particularly so in the case of Iraq.

This was a highly successful approach, Marshall suggests, with neoconservatives able to 'secure nearly total control of all aspects of policy surrounding the war and the subsequent occupation.'[36] In this line of reasoning, investigating Bush's beliefs is a side-show as he effectively held no beliefs, allowing his savvy advisors to do

whatever they liked in his name. If this is the case, then investigating Bush's personality as a key influence on the doctrine is unimportant, except to the extent that the
image of him as a delegator would be reinforced.

However, on close examination the argument that Bush was simply a puppet
of neoconservatives, rather than an independent decision-making force, is problematic. Robert Kagan notes a difficulty with the dominance-of-mid-level-officials
argument: 'As a purely practical matter, the suggestion has always presented a
puzzle. How did they do it?'[37] The famous neoconservative Richard Perle, when the
Marshall thesis was put to him, found it 'wildly off the mark. It doesn't say who the
neoconservatives are. There were only a handful, they were far from the most influential [people within the administration], and they didn't hold the same views on a
number of aspects of post-9/11 foreign policy.'[38]

Paul Wolfowitz is often cited as being at the core of this group. However,
Wolfowitz was not regarded by neo-cons as a particularly devout parishioner.
Joshua Muravchik, an influential neoconservative writer and a major proponent of
democracy promotion, explained:

> Neo-cons are a bunch of writers and intellectuals. Paul has always been in government
> service, and… the whole métier of neo-cons is to carry arguments with a vigor that is
> not acceptable for those inside the government, and so Paul has never participated in
> that. I think he's on the same side as us, but I always thought of Paul as sort a neo-con
> fellow traveler, someone on the inside who sympathized with us, but would never go as
> far, or speak as bluntly. Paul has never had a special interest in the democracy agenda. He's
> always been supportive of it [but] Paul's shtick has always been military issues.[39]

Douglas Feith was often grouped with Perle and Wolfowitz as part of the neo-con
cadre. Feith's memoir – not a forum in which the protagonist customarily under-
plays their influence – details his role in the policy process as being what one would
expect of a second-tier official; writing concept papers, attending Deputies' committee meetings, and carrying out assignments given him by Rumsfeld.

In this context, Feith's account of the provenance of the 'war on terror' frame
is significant. Although neoconservatives such as Feith are sometimes credited
with framing post-9/11 foreign policy as a war against terrorism, rather than as a
set of law-enforcement actions, as Feith has it he was in Moscow when he received
news of the September 11th attacks. Feith heard Bush's initial response – 'Terrorism
against our nation will not stand' – and took this as the president signalling that he
considered this to be a matter of war, not law enforcement. Feith regarded this as
'strategic guidance' for the memos he was preparing for Rumsfeld.[40] The next day,
Feith, another neo-con Peter Rodman, and Generals Abizaid and Luti boarded a US
military plane to return to Washington. For much of the flight, the four:

> [S]tood together in the middle of the plane discussing what it would mean for the United
> States to be at war. Even as we deliberated, President Bush confirmed in a late morning

statement that he viewed the previous day's attacks as 'war'. The KC-135 was not set up for real-time communications, so we didn't learn this until we landed. But the President's initial statement had persuaded us that he was treating the attack as an act of war, not just a crime.[41]

The war on terror frame – perhaps the key element of the Bush doctrine – came from the president and guided Feith's input into the policymaking process, rather than the other way around.

Moreover, the democratization agenda was one that had always split the neoconservatives, and so it is difficult to see Bush as simply mirroring the views of a monolithic neo-con movement on this issue. Jeanne Kirkpatrick, considered a founding figure of the neoconservative movement, was very sceptical of promoting democracy in Iraq. Her seminal essay, 'Dictatorships and Double Standards', had argued that while totalitarian regimes were mortal threats to the US and should be opposed, merely authoritarian regimes could be useful allies. Policies which embarrassed or punished authoritarian allies of the United States, such as those she identified at the time with President Carter, were injurious to national security and harmed the more important fight against totalitarianism.[42]

Francis Fukayama, who argued in 1989 that democracy's triumph in the world of ideas would inevitably be translated to the world of the material, has stressed that he did not consider it appropriate for the United States to act as the 'vanguard of the party' on this issue, nudging the material world along:

> The United States does not get to decide when and where democracy comes about. By definition, outsiders can't 'impose' democracy on a country that doesn't want it; demand for democracy and reform must be domestic. Democracy promotion is therefore a long-term and opportunistic process that has to await the gradual ripening of political and economic conditions to be effective.[43]

'I think there is a pretty broad consensus', Richard Perle says, 'that promotion of democracy should be part of American policy.' But how central a part? 'Where the question gets interesting,' Perle continued in a vein similar to Kirkpatrick's argument:

> [I]s in how do you reconcile the desire to encourage democratic institutions with the sometimes necessity of working with dictators, because you have interests that trump your interest in democracy? The caricature of neo-conservatism is people who are blind to the compromises that have to be made, because we are not living in a world in which we can afford to have a single goal, or a goal so dominant that everything else is subordinated to it, independent of circumstances. So, that's where you get the division. Now some people are more passionate about it, and are willing to try even in circumstances that look pretty dismal. Others think it's a desirable idea, but they are not prepared to expend a lot of time or money or political capital to achieve it.[44]

President Bush, of course, would signal a commitment to spend almost all of his foreign policy capital on the goal of ending tyranny and promoting democracy. Secretary Rumsfeld felt democracy promotion to be desirable but very difficult to achieve and not worth the expenditure of huge resources.

Bush, then, endorsed some ideas associated with neoconservatives, in particular pre-emption, although the evidence is that he was attracted to them as they fit his temperament or because he independently reached conclusions that were congruent with neoconservatives. On democratization, Bush's black-and-white moralism and history-making temperament led him to embrace this cause more fully even than neoconservatives such as Kirkpatrick, Kristol, Perle, and Feith. Cheney, as discussed above, and Rumsfeld, as discussed below, were uncomfortable with the democracy agenda, whilst Rumsfeld also had severe doubts about pre-emption and the entire war on terror concept. The president's temperament and personality seems more important in shaping the Bush doctrine than the writings and advocacy of neoconservative intellectuals and officials.[45]

Why not another worldview?

There were alternative worldviews to which the president might have turned following 9/11. If other strategies were possible under the circumstances, and Bush did not choose them, then we have a stronger case that the environment was malleable enough to succumb to the influence of the individual.

First, the president could have continued the conventionally realist policies of his early administration. Rogue states could be contained, as these weak dictatorships would eventually collapse due to their internal pathologies. In the meantime, deterrence would suffice to prevent rogue state aggression, whilst an enhancement of counter-proliferation instruments would retard the spread of weapons of mass destruction. Existing alliance relationships could be strengthened, drawing on an increase in goodwill and a new appreciation of shared threat amongst regional allies. The old policy of working with friendly autocrats in the Middle East could be re-endorsed, with additional pressure brought to bear on regimes such as Saudi Arabia to re-double the efforts of their security services in capturing terrorists within their borders.[46]

This seemed inadequate to Bush. Realists stress the impossibility of achieving perfect security or eradicating all enemies. Instead, vigilant maintenance of a credible deterrent posture, and adroit management of alliances, can reduce the overall level of threat and keep conflict to a minimum. But at the core of realism is the need for cool compromises on morality and on the possibility of achieving perfect security, and compromise did not appeal to the president in these circumstances. Moreover, realism was an approach closely associated with the foreign policies of the George H.W. Bush administration, which the younger Bush viewed as unambitious. A persuasive case could be made, Bush believed, that it was decades of stability-focused realist policies that had brought about the terrorist problem to begin with.

Second, the president could have adopted the liberal internationalist frame-work offered by the British prime minister. Tony Blair, fearing that the result of 9/11 could be that 'the Americans jump out of the international system', proposed to the president that the response be internationalized and focused on eradicating poverty and desperation as the root causes of the terrorist impulses.[47] The major focus, after an Afghanistan campaign carried out by a multi-national coalition, should be a re-engagement in the Middle East peace process. With a genuine attempt to solve this issue well underway, then the effort to address other regional problems – such as Saddam Hussein – would begin from a basis of international consensus and the moral high ground.[48]

Bush rejected this approach. The diplomacy needed to build a wide-ranging coalition would introduce delay and uncertainty. The Middle East peace process had been recently pushed by President Clinton to little effect. The emphasis on poverty as a root cause of terrorism was over-thinking the problem, Bush thought. In the president's worldview, good and evil were irreducible givens, rather than learned behaviours, and so the root cause of evil was evil itself. As Douglas Feith notes:

> [C]uring poverty and solving the Arab-Israeli conflict were worthy goals even aside from the war on terrorism … but in practice such talk of 'root causes' tended to produce paralysis rather than motivate action against terrorist extremist ideology… so it was unconstructive, to say the least, to give up on fighting terrorist ideology until we had cured world poverty or solved the Palestine problem – goals we could hardly count on reaching soon, if ever.[49]

Third, the president could have turned America inwards after 9/11, adopting a policy of retrenchment. Various forms of this were available. Henry Nau, describing alternative conservative responses to 9/11, identifies a 'nationalist' wing that would prefer to 'concentrate on homeland defense and let allies in Europe and Asia assume greater responsibility' for dealing with regional problems such as Iraq and North Korea.[50] Letting others deal with problems was an appealing principle to Rumsfeld. Retrenchment was also a policy advocated by some realists, following the logic of John Mearsheimer's argument that the most sensible strategy for a great power surrounded by oceans is to act as an 'offshore balancer'.[51]

To Bush, this would be a tacit acknowledgement of defeat. As historian John Lewis Gaddis has noted, the American experience has been to respond to exter-nal threats by adopting a greater rather than lesser world role.[52] Gaddis received the presidential Medal of Freedom and had some contact with the White House after making this argument, suggesting his ideas were well received.

Other strategies, then, were available to the United States following 9/11, but these strategies were not consistent with the president's temperament and personality. The Bush doctrine of pre-emption, black-and-white framing of issues, and the democracy agenda was congruent with the president's proclivities, and so the individual, here, is an indispensable part of the explanation. Another individual in Bush's place may very well have laid out a different strategic course.

Donald Rumsfeld and the Bush doctrine

Donald Rumsfeld reacted to the 9/11 shock very differently than Bush. Rumsfeld had been thinking about foreign policy for decades, was deeply experienced, and had a well-worked-out philosophy.[53] Moreover, Rumsfeld brought an entirely different disposition to the task. He saw the world as much less amenable to reshaping, and was not interested in grand moralistic schemes.

Indeed, Rumsfeld was not enamoured of doctrinal pronouncements in general. As he put it in his memoirs:

> I have found that there often seem to be exceptions even to the wisest of doctrines. It is appealing to seek simplicity and relief from the burdens and risks of continually having to make difficult judgment calls. Faced with major decisions, senior officials – military and civilian – need to be careful not to follow doctrine mechanically instead of engaging their judgments.[54]

On 9/11, whilst Bush's instincts ran to talk of basic good and evil, Rumsfeld was analytical. In his memoir, the secretary juxtaposes the president's comments to the principals on 9/11 with his own cooler commentary. Bush, on a video-link from Offutt Air Force Base, said 'No thugs are going to diminish the spirit of the United States. No coward is going to hold this government at bay. We're going to find out who did this. We're going to destroy them.'[55] Rumsfeld's advice had a different cast:

> I...advised the president in the days following that I believed our nation's response should not primarily be about punishment, retribution, or retaliation. Punishing our enemies didn't describe the range of actions we would need to take if we were to succeed in protecting the United States. Our responsibility was to deter and dissuade others from thinking that terrorism against the United States could advance their cause. In my view, our principal motivation was self-defense, not vengeance, retaliation, or punishment.[56]

Where Bush sought certainty, Rumsfeld found the post-9/11 period 'a time of discovery – of seeking elusive, imperfect solutions to problems that would not be solved quickly. There was no guidebook or road map for us to follow.'[57] He disliked the term war on terror, and wrote several memos suggesting it be modified or abandoned.[58] The term 'war' gave an inaccurate impression that the response would be solely military, whilst 'terror' was, Rumsfeld believed, a feeling or a tactic rather than an enemy. Bush decided against Rumsfeld and preferred the straightforward nature of the war on terror tag.[59]

Contrary to popular belief, Rumsfeld was not a strong force behind the decision to invade Iraq. The national security team met four days after the 9/11 attacks to consider the US response, and the issue of war on Iraq was raised by Paul Wolfowitz. A vote of the principals was 4–0 against. Rumsfeld abstained. Colin Powell found this to be characteristic of Rumsfeld. According to Bob Woodward's account, 'Powell found Rumsfeld's abstention most interesting. What did it mean? Rumsfeld had this way of asking questions, questions, questions! – and not revealing his own position.'[60] In his memoirs, Rumsfeld recalls that 'I supported military action against Al-Qaeda and the Taliban because they left us no alternative. Saddam, in my mind, was different. I thought we might be able to find other ways of bringing about regime change in Iraq.'[61] It might be worthwhile, he wrote in a memo to himself, 'to give Saddam Hussein a way out for his family to live in comfort.'[62]

Rumsfeld had little role in shaping the rhetoric or underlying policy behind the 'axis of evil' approach. He later recalled that the speech was 'not particularly in my area.'[63] Asked about another key question of the period – should the US take the Iraq issue to the UN – Rumsfeld also claimed no strong views.

Rumsfeld's view on pre-emption was also non-doctrinaire – one had to know the specific circumstances. He told Woodward that the doctrine went back to the sixteenth century and Sir Thomas More's *Utopia*. The key question was the intelligence on the imminence of the threat: 'What information would you require, and with what degree of certainty, before you launched a preemptive attack?'[64] The secretary's approach to the issue of democracy promotion was close to a classical realist position – a country's internal politics were their own business, the issue was whether they were helpful or injurious to US interests:

> Instead of labeling countries as good or bad – democratic or nondemocratic, pro-human rights or anti-human rights – I thought a better way of categorizing countries was to consider the direction in which they were heading. If a country that had been a long-time abuser of human rights and a foe of democracy was making steps toward freer political and economic systems, I believed we should calculate whether continued progress in the right direction was likelier to be achieved by encouraging rather than publicly chiding its leadership. I recognized the US interest – practical as well as moral – in having other countries respect basic human rights and function democratically. But I saw that interest of ours as one of several that needed to be considered in the making of US policy. It was not the sole interest, and it did not necessarily trump all others.[65]

Rumsfeld's approach to this issue was in stark contrast to that of the president. 'If we took on such a good and evil view of the world, we wouldn't be able to count on support from any non-democratic country.'[66] Douglas Feith reports that he and Rumsfeld exerted some effort to have the president tone down his democracy rhetoric: 'The proper way to think about this, we believed, was that the Iraqis would have to *create their own democracy*.'; 'Democracy is complex,' Rumsfeld argued in principals committee meetings prior to the war, 'it is a lot more than just organizing an election.'[67]

The US strategic response to 9/11 was strongly conditioned by who the president was. Another leader, in Bush's place, would have responded differently. Rumsfeld did not respond to 9/11 in the same way as Bush. The Bush doctrine, then, is well named – it was a very personal strategic framework born of the interaction between the president's temperament, worldview, and the shock of 9/11. Rumsfeld, though, did decisively shape the next part of the story: planning for the invasion of Iraq.

Notes

1 See Robert Jervis, 'Understanding the Bush Doctrine', *Political Science Quarterly*, 118 (2003): 365–388; Ivo H. Daalder and James M. Lindsay, *America Unbound: The Bush Revolution in Foreign Policy* (Washington, D.C.: Brookings Institution Press, 2003); and Stanley A. Renshon and Peter Suedfeld, *Understanding the Bush Doctrine: Psychology and Strategy in an Age of Terrorism* (New York: Taylor & Francis, 2007).

2 On this point, see Jervis, 'Understanding the Bush Doctrine', 372.

3 William Langley, 'Revealed: What Really Went on During Bush's Missing Hours', *Daily Telegraph*, 16 December 2001, www.telegraph.co.uk/news/worldnews/northamerica/usa/1365455/Revealed-what-really-went-on-during-Bushs-missing-hours.html.

4 An analogous example of the lived experience of crisis prompting belief system change can be found in James G. Blight, *The Shattered Crystal Ball: Fear and Learning in the Cuban Missile Crisis* (Baltimore, MD: Rowman and Littlefield, 1992).

5 Langley, 'Revealed…'.

6 Dan Balz and Bob Woodward, 'Bush's Global Strategy Began to Take Shape in First Frantic Hours After Attack', *Washington Post*, 27 January 2002, www.washingtonpost.com/wp-dyn/articles/A42754-2002Jan26.html.

7 George W. Bush, *Decision Points* (New York: Broadway, 2011), 127.

8 Langley, 'Revealed…'.

9 Langley, 'Revealed…'; Bush's statement: www.presidency.ucsb.edu/ws/index.php?pid=58055&st=&st1=#.

10 Balz and Woodward, 'Bush's global strategy…'.

11 Langley, 'Revealed…'.

12 Balz and Woodward, 'Bush's global strategy…'.

13 Bush, *Decision Points*, 128.

14 President's statement: www.presidency.ucsb.edu/ws/index.php?pid=58056&st=&st1=.

15 National Commission on Terrorist Attacks on the United States, '9/11 Commission Final Report,' available at www.9-11commission.gov/report/911Report.pdf.

16 George W. Bush Address to the Nation on the Terrorist Attacks, available at www.presidency.ucsb.edu/ws/index.php?pid=58057&st=&st1=.

17 Balz and Woodward, 'Bush's global strategy…'.

18 George W. Bush, 'Address Before a Joint Session of Congress on the State of the Union', 29 January 2002. Available at www.presidency.ucsb.edu/ws/index.php?pid=29644&st=&st1=#axzz1TcOWxaX6.

19 George W. Bush, 'Statement Before a Joint Session of Congress on the State of the Union', 28 January 2003, available at www.presidency.ucsb.edu/ws/index.php?pid=29645&st=&st1=.

20 Frank Bruni, 'For President, a Mission and a Role in History', *New York Times*, 22 September 2001. www.nytimes.com/2001/09/22/us/nation-challenged-white-house-memo-for-president-mission-role-history.html.

21 George W. Bush, 'Commencement Address at the United States Military Academy in West Point, New York', 1 June 2002. Available at www.presidency.ucsb.edu/ws/index.php?pid=62730&st=&st1=.

22 Although, in later years, the Bush and Obama administrations would attempt to create deterrent threats against terrorist groups, seeking to create the perception that attacks could fail, or prestige be lost, for example, as analogies to the cold war deterrent threat against territory. See Eric Schmitt and Thom Shanker, *Counterstrike: The Untold Story of America's Secret Campaign Against Al Qaeda* (New York: St. Martins, 2012).

23 Robert Jervis, 'The Confrontation Between the US and Iraq: Implications for the Theory and Practice of Deterrence', *European Journal of International Relations* 9. (2003): 315–337.

24 Bruni, 'For President, a Mission…'.

25 Bruni, 'For President, a Mission…'.

26 Barton Gellman, *Angler: The Cheney Vice Presidency* (New York: Penguin, 2008) 250–251.

27 Quoted in Amy Zegard, 'The Legend of a Democracy Promoter', *The National Interest* 97 (2008) 51.

28 Author interview with Wehner.

29 Author interview with Wehner.

30 Author interview with Cohen.

31 Bing West, *The Strongest Tribe: War, Politics, and the Endgame in Iraq* (New York: Random House), 64, 71.

32 Scott McClellan, *What Happened: Inside the Bush White House and Washington's Culture of Deception* (New York: Public Affairs, 2008), 197.

33 Jay Nordlinger, 'Being Sharansky', *National Review* (2005) available at http://nrd.national-review.com/article/?q=Yzc4NzdmZDk0M2NmZTZkODUyMzllNjZlYmU3ZWJkNmQ.

34 Interview information.

35 Author interview with Wehner.

36 Joshua Micah Marshall, 'Remaking the World: Bush and the Neoconservatives', *Foreign Affairs* 82 (2003) 6.

37 Robert Kagan, 'Neocon Nation: Neoconservatism c. 1776', *World Affairs* (2008) available at www.worldaffairsjournal.org/2008%20-%20Spring/full-neocon.html.

38 Author interview with Perle.

39 Author interview with Muravchik.

40 Douglas Feith, *War and Decision: Inside the Pentagon at the Dawn of the War on Terror* (New York: Harper, 2008), 3.

41 Feith, *War and Decision*, 5–6.

42 Jeanne Kirkpatrick, 'Dictatorships and Double Standards', *Commentary*, November 1979, available at www.commentarymagazine.com/viewarticle.cfm/dictatorships--double-standards-6189.

43 Francis Fukayama, 'After Neo-conservatism', *New York Times*, 9 February 2006, available at www.nytimes.com/2006/02/19/magazine/neo.html?ei=5090&en=4126fa38fefd80de&ex=1298005200&partner=rssuserland&emc=rss&pagewanted=all.

44 Author interview with Perle.

45 See also Timothy J. Lynch, 'Did Bush Pursue a Neoconservative Foreign Policy?' in Iwan W. Morgan and Philip Davies, eds, *Assessing George W. Bush's Legacy: The Right Man?* (Basingstoke: Palgrave-Macmillan, 2010), 121–144.

46 For an elucidation of a post-9/11 realist strategy, see Stephen Walt 'Beyond Bin Laden: Reshaping US Foreign Policy', *International Security* 26 (2001–2002), 56–78. For a discussion of differences between realism and neoconservatism, see Brian C. Schmidt and Michael C. Williams, 'The Bush Doctrine and the Iraq War: Neoconservatives Versus Realists', *Security Studies* 17 (2008), 191–220.

47 See Stephen Benedict Dyson, *The Blair Identity: Leadership and Foreign Policy* (Manchester: Manchester University Press, 2009).

48 Dyson, *The Blair Identity*, 70–74.

49 Feith, *War and Decision*, 170–171.

50 Henry Nau, 'No Enemies on the Right: Conservative Foreign Policy Factions Beyond Iraq', *The National Interest* (Winter 2004/05), 22.

51 See Walt, 'Beyond Bin Laden', 75.

52 John Lewis Gaddis, *Surprise, Security, and the American Experience* (Cambridge, MA: Harvard University Press, 2004).

53 Ann Scott Tyson, 'Rumsfeld's Worldview: a Ruthless Place', *Christian Science Monitor*, 93 (2001): 1.

54 Donald H. Rumsfeld, *Known and Unknown* (New York: Sentinel, 2011), 438.

55 Rumsfeld, *Known and Unknown*, 343.

56 Rumsfeld, *Known and Unknown*, 343.

57 Rumsfeld, *Known and Unknown*, 352.

58 Donald Rumsfeld to George W. Bush, 'Global War on Terror', 18 June 2004. http://library.Rumsfeld.com/doclib/sp/261/To%20President%20George%20W.%20Bush%20re%20Global%20War%20on%20Terror-%20Memo%20Attachment%2006-18-2004.pdf#search="global war on terror".

59 Rumsfeld, *Known and Unknown*, 353.

60 Bob Woodward, *Plan of Attack* (New York: Simon & Schuster, 2004), 25.

61 Rumsfeld, *Known and Unknown*.

62 Rumsfeld, 'Saddam Hussein', 21 September 2001. http://library.Rumsfeld.com/doclib/sp/295/Re%20Saddam%20Hussein%2009-21-2001.pdf.

63 Woodward, *Plan of Attack*, 96.

64 Woodward, *Plan of Attack*, 133.

65 Rumsfeld, *Known and Unknown*, 632.

66 Rumsfeld, *Known and Unknown*, 634.

67 Feith, *War and Decision*, 284–286, 287.

4

Rumsfeld and the invasion plan

Considered in isolation from what came later, the invasion plan for Iraq was daring in conception, achieved its goals with stunning speed and at low cost, and represented a sparkling advertisement for Rumsfeld's vision of a light, fast army. Planning saw close interaction between Rumsfeld and Gen. Tommy Franks, showing the positive potential of Rumsfeld's leadership style. The secretary was insistent, questioning and effective in shaping a plan that married Franks' war-fighting expertise with the goals of the civilian Pentagon leadership. Instead of crumpling before Rumsfeld or ignoring him, Franks took the secretary's incessant questioning as a positive cue, and together they fashioned an effective product. The positive impact of Rumsfeld on the invasion plan serves as a useful reminder that studies of controversial leaders should take account of the upside, as well as the downside, of each worldview and decision style.

This episode shows the good side of Rumsfeld's leadership style. However, his insistent questioning of Franks was confined to the invasion plan. He asked relatively few questions about post-war planning, and the operation would have benefited greatly from an in-depth probe of assumptions and contingencies about the aftermath. Rumsfeld, though, did not believe the US should be involved in Iraqi affairs after the overthrow of Saddam.

The president, by contrast, did believe that the US should shape a democratic post-Saddam Iraq. However, he engaged with the war plan only sporadically and superficially, delegating the work to Franks and the supervision to Rumsfeld. In this episode, it was the delegatory side of Bush's style that dominated his approach to policy.

Table 4.1 provides an overview of the impact of Bush and Rumsfeld on this period of Iraq decision making and the remainder of the chapter traces the manner in which their styles shaped policy.

Rumsfeld and Franks

Rumsfeld's association with Franks began with the Afghanistan war. Initial impressions were not good. Franks, as with many of the military officers with whom

Table 4.1   Bush, Rumsfeld and the war plan

Bush's traits	The war plan	Rumsfeld's traits	The war plan
Black-and-white worldview		Complex worldview	War planning begins from fundamental assumptions. Focus on the unpredictable and the unknowable.
History maker		History manager	Post-war stability not US concern.
Cheerleading interpersonal style	Bolsters rather than questions Franks.	Prosecutorial interpersonal style	Tense but effective planning process with Gen. Franks.
Delegator	War planning delegated almost entirely to Rumsfeld/Franks.	Dictator or delegator?	Prodded and cajoled Franks, neither delegating to him nor issuing him direct orders.

Rumsfeld interacted, initially resented the secretary's aggressive questioning. However, unlike many officers who fumed in silence, Franks did the more effective thing, which was to stand his ground. 'Mr. Secretary, stop,' he said to Rumsfeld as the Afghanistan war was being planned in late September 2001. 'This isn't going to work. You can fire me. I'm either the commander or I'm not, and you've got to trust me or you don't.'[1] As Rumsfeld put it in his memoirs, 'It took some time for us to get used to each other. My habit of asking probing questions was new to Franks; he needed to become comfortable with my queries and confident of my regard for him.'[2]

Franks was also resistant at first to Rumsfeld's transformational approach to warfare, based upon speed, agility, precision weaponry and unconventional thinking. But Franks' experience in Afghanistan – the iconic image of which was special operatives on horseback acting as spotters for laser-guided missiles – made him a convert. Rumsfeld moulded Franks into a general who was creative in terms of doctrine and from whom he could expect a constructive reaction to questions. Former House Speaker Newt Gingrich, who as a member of the Defence Policy Board knew both men and observed their interaction, felt the relationship was 'fraught with creative tension. Franks understood that Rumsfeld would throw ideas at him and would grill him about any and every aspect of his plan. Rumsfeld knew there was a line beyond which Franks could not be pushed.' Gingrich characterized it as 'constant negotiation.'[3] The result, though, was positive. The process, Franks recalled, 'Caused me to respect him a lot. And you ought to ask him if he respects me. My guess is he'd probably say that he does.'[4]

Pentagon aides characterized the Rumsfeld-Franks planning process as 'an exercise in suasion'. As Gordon and Trainor put it, 'Rumsfeld never directed Franks on how to write the plan. But he would plant ideas, send concepts and papers his way, and ask questions to shape the plan.'[5] Rumsfeld's close aide Lawrence Di Rita explained the process:

> Rumsfeld, in contrast to the impression of him as a command-and-control kind of guy giving orders, that's not the way he operated. He liked decisions to surface through a process of consensus discussion, and this whole idea of iterations in planning [for the invasion] was all to do with ensuring that the system was fully massaged before anything came from it. So he spent a lot of time driving consensus in decision making. And that was sometimes frustrating for the Department of Defense in particular, because military people generally are not trained to push back on civilian authority, and Rumsfeld depended upon that. And so sometimes what was perceived as provocation was actually an attempt to stimulate discussion.[6]

Principles of planning

Prior to 9/11, Rumsfeld had begun a process of reviewing all of the plans for possible US war-fighting operations around the world – not only Iraq but also other potential problem areas such as North Korea. He saw shortcomings in the plans. They conceptualized the US military, Rumsfeld thought, as a blunt instrument rather than a precision tool. They were prescriptions for full-scale war using overwhelming force, reflecting the dominant influence of the Powell doctrine. Little flexibility was available: 'Either it's world peace or it's World War III. Either the switch is off or it's on.'[7]

The plans were also old, failing to reflect changed circumstances in the countries in question and in US doctrine and military capability. Revision was slow and bureaucratic – usually taking two or three years to completely redesign a war plan. Because of this, the incentives for the military were to stick with the basis of an existing plan and make changes only around the margins. Rumsfeld wanted more flexibility: 'We owe the country and the president war plans, contingency plans, thinking that is current. And the only way we're going to get that is if we can compress that process dramatically and shorten it from years down to some cycle so that it can be refreshed with current assumptions.'[8]

The secretary began calling in the combatant commanders to refresh all plans, making sure that each began with a careful consideration of the underlying assumptions:

> I believed that key assumptions needed to be the foundation of any contingency plan, but I had found that military planners did not always cite them or give them the probing,

intense consideration they merited. In meetings at the Pentagon, I emphasized that failing to examine the assumptions on which a plan is based can start a planning process based on incorrect premises, and then proceed logically to incorrect conclusions.[9]

This was enormously frustrating to busy general officers who felt they already had workable plans for most contingencies. Considering foundational assumptions in an abstract context, whilst under withering questioning from the secretary of defence, was not a prospect they relished, especially as Rumsfeld insisted on conducting the exercise on a sweltering Saturday in peacetime August 2001.[10]

The unmistakable signals were that Rumsfeld would be breaking with traditional planning processes, that he expected new and creative thinking, and that he was determined to play a close personal role in shaping assumptions and in taking those assumptions forward into operational plans. Franks wisely noted this, and adopted Rumsfeld's approach to problems. The secretary was insistent on seeing not only plans, but the assumptions that underlay the plans. Franks made a point of always including briefing slides laying out in detail the assumptions that underlay his more specific planning work.

Iterations

The general review of plans became, after 9/11, a very specific exercise in revising the Iraq invasion scenario. Planning began on Wednesday 21 November 2001, when Bush asked Rumsfeld 'How do you feel about the war plan for Iraq?'[11] Rumsfeld reported that he was unhappy with it, and was already moving to refresh all of the Pentagon's war plans. Rumsfeld now tasked Franks with moving forward rapidly on Iraq planning.

The first step was for Franks to work on a 'commander's concept': a broad overview of strategy but not yet an executable plan. Franks indicated that the existing war plan for Iraq – 'Op Plan 1003' – did not fit the secretary's goals for transformational warfare. Op Plan 1003 was essentially a formula for re-fighting the first Gulf War which had, after all, been spectacularly successful from an American military standpoint. To Rumsfeld, though, it was unsatisfactory. Op Plan 1003 relied upon the Powell doctrine principles of a long, slow build-up of a large, overwhelming ground force, which would idle in the desert for a prolonged period whilst an extensive air campaign softened up Iraqi resistance. Franks called it a 'no-risk plan' that involved 'a whole bunch of divisions, a whole bunch of jets, a whole bunch of bombs, a whole bunch of aircraft carriers.'[12] To Rumsfeld,

> It was only a slightly modified version of the one used during the first Gulf War. It called for roughly the same number of forces used then – nearly half a million US troops to be marshaled into the region over many months. They were to invade through Iraq's southern desert, much as they had in 1991. Because the firepower and precision of US forces had increased substantially since then, the plan would represent a vastly more lethal force

in 2003. Someone in the briefing described the plan, appropriately I thought, as 'Desert Storm on steroids'.[13]

Not only had US munitions grown much more potent, Saddam's forces had become much weaker. And in 1991, 'enormous quantities of equipment and other materiel sent to the Gulf were never used'. This was an offence to Rumsfeld's principles of efficiency.[14]

Talking points for an early Rumsfeld-Franks meeting on the Iraq plan showcased the principles the secretary valued: 'Surprise, speed, shock and risk'. The US should 'be ready to strike from a standing start', and go with a smaller number of forces initially with 'large forces [to] flow in behind'. What was required of Franks, at this stage, was a 'rough concept, not complete execution-level planning'.[15] Rumsfeld wanted a plan he could help shape, not a finished product that he had to accept or reject.

Franks, working from these instructions, developed his commander's concept and briefed it to the president on 28 December. Franks had constructed a matrix of 'lines of operation' that made extensive use of precision munitions and US speed and expertise, great advantages for what would be a numerically inferior force. The lines were plotted against targets of regime vulnerability, which Franks termed 'slices' – such as the leadership, the Iraqi internal security apparatus, and the commercial and economic infrastructure. Little starbursts indicated which 'lines of operation' could be brought to bear against which 'slices' of vulnerability.[16] The overall effect was to create a matrix of flexible and creative ways to bring pressure to bear on the Saddam regime during the invasion, avoiding the massive employment of blunt force and consequent long period of building up troops and supplies.

Rumsfeld was pleased. Franks had even listed the assumptions underlying his thinking. Some were banal ('CENTCOM would have sufficient munitions') and some turned out to be mistaken ('Iraq possessed WMD capability, so the US would have to plan to fight against it'.) But Rumsfeld appreciated that Franks had taken on board his planning methods and laid out the logic underlying the plans.[17]

Rumsfeld responded to Franks' 'lines and slices' briefing with a list of new questions for the general. They required a huge effort to answer, but were also a spur to further refinement of the plan. Among the most significant:

- Exactly how much had the Iraqi military been degraded since the Gulf War in 1991?
- [With reference to the lines and slices matrix] What were the meaningful targets? How long would it take to have the effect you want on those targets?
- If dozens of key targets could be destroyed simultaneously, would that put pressure on the regime, cause it to crumble and preclude the need for a long war requiring a large force?[18]

The secretary was determined to keep pushing Franks' in the direction of speed, agility and a smaller force. Franks responded well. His chief deputy, Gene Renuart, was irked, finding the questions to be an unwelcome burden. But Franks had learned by now how to work with Rumsfeld. 'Here's the deal, so let's not try to fight the wrong fight … let's fight in the direction we need to go together.' In other words: answer Rumsfeld's questions.[19]

Three iterations of planning unfurled.[20] In the first, the overall concept of the war was termed the *generated start*. A long build-up would allow staging of the entire invasion force prior to the commencement of hostilities. Rumsfeld thought the approach ponderous. He was also uncomfortable with the separation of a period of 'shaping' operations from the air from the commencement of decisive ground operations. Rather than ordering Franks to change the concept, Rumsfeld asked the general a question that would push him in the desired direction. What, Rumsfeld wanted to know, would be the US response if Saddam took precipitate action, such as shooting down a US plane or torching his oil fields, whilst the US was engaging in the long build-up? In Woodward's words, Rumsfeld was asking 'What could surprise them? What had they overlooked, not anticipated? There were so many variables and unknowns. What was it they were not seeing that was in front of their eyes? Saddam's propensity and ability to provoke in a major way was a "known unknown".'[21]

Franks and his team incorporated Rumsfeld's thoughts into a new option, the *running start*. The US would initiate war with a baseline of forces, prior to the arrival of additional strength. The plan would rely on speed of advance to pressure the regime and keep Iraqi defences off balance, whilst reinforcements flowed in behind to consolidate the advantage.[22] The evolution over the generated start was that war could begin without the whole force in place.

Running Start became the conceptual basis for the final US war plan.[23] Franks had embraced Rumsfeld's tutelage on force size. He commented that 'I believe it is probable that just driving a division and an MEB (Marine Expeditionary Brigade) into Iraq will cause it to implode.'[24] However, when the US Central Command (CENTCOM) staff war-gamed Running Start in December, they determined that the force was too light and would be in danger of becoming bogged down, unable to exploit initial gains due to insufficient numbers. Franks was persuaded by these concerns, but indicated that Rumsfeld's voice would be decisive. On 12 December, Rumsfeld was briefed by Franks and the CENTCOM staff, and he accepted the need for a larger force.[25] Rumsfeld was not against accepting reasonable arguments – backed by data – that suggested that his assumptions required modification.

The final plan, then, represented a compromise between Rumsfeld's original vision of a lean, fast force, and the concerns of CENTCOM on troop numbers. The compromise was this: If the initial deployment was able to decisively defeat Saddam, all the better. But if not, overwhelming force would be flowing in behind. According to Franks: 'If the cost begins to approach a gamble, then you put in the pipeline forces, which guarantee success in the event you've miscalculated with the start force.'[26] The air and ground campaigns would commence simultaneously, in a shift away from Powell doctrine era operations.

As the official army history put it:

> With a clear understanding of the strategic situation and of the CFLCC's combat power, General Franks made the deliberate decision to start the ground fight before some of the designated forces were available and ready for combat. He balanced the strategic, operational, and tactical benefits of a rapid, early advance against the risk inherent in not having sufficient combat power to achieve the campaign's objective at the start of operations.[27]

Balancing risk was, of course, a mantra of Rumsfeld's as he sought to overturn what he saw as the excessively cautious Powell doctrine of overwhelming force. And it was at least initially successful:

> Violating virtually all of the traditional wisdom about how to prepare for a campaign of this scope, the V Corps and 1 MEF forces [the main units of the US invasion] appear to have achieved operational and tactical surprise when they started their attack before all of the 'necessary' forces had arrived and without a lengthy air effort. Accepting the inherent risks, General Franks and Lieutenant General McKiernan understood the necessity and value of attacking early and aggressively. The running start appears to have thrown the Iraqis off of their defensive plan, and they were never able to regain their footing. Coalition forces moved farther and faster than any Iraqi – and even many in the coalition – believed possible.[28]

Rumsfeld had insisted upon the identification of 'off ramps' where the flow of forces into Iraq could be halted. The analogy in the secretary's mind was the corporate principle of 'just-in-time' logistics, where the flow of inventory was carefully monitored so that valuable goods were not left rotting in a warehouse. Rumsfeld disliked the system for coordinating deployment of troops and material, known as the Time-Phased Force and Deployment List (TPFDL). He believed that it scheduled the deployment of assets too far in advance. As then Army Secretary Thomas White puts it, 'The secretary of defense is a micro-manager by nature. He did not like the notion that he would make an initial decision to deploy a force, and that beyond that initial decision, the rest of it would kind of be on automatic pilot.'[29]

Rumsfeld turned off the flow of additional forces once it became clear that the regime was falling under the pressure of the initial deployment. But the armed forces were reliant on the precise programming of the TPFDL to such an extent that the logistical losses, in terms of misplaced supplies and the cancelling of seemingly-peripheral-yet-actually-crucial deployments outweighed the gains. As the army history of the war records, 'concepts such as "just-in-time logistics" briefed better than they performed'.[30]

The successful overthrow of the Saddam Hussein regime was achieved in just 21 days, and few of the horrific predictions of a scorched-earth retreat, the use of WMD, or a 'Saddamgrad' urban-nightmare defence of Baghdad transpired. The coalition loss rate was less than one in 2,300, amongst the lowest in the history of modern warfare. By any measure, this was a major military accomplishment.[31] According to military historian John Keegan, the principles stressed by Rumsfeld were a key reason for the success:

> Superior equipment and organization supplied many of the reasons why such success had been won. Besides material and technical factors, however, moral and psychological dimensions had been at work. Daring and boldness had played parts in the campaign as significant as dominance in the air, greater firepower, or higher mobility on the ground.[32]

The president and the war plan

Bush had delegated the war planning to Rumsfeld. Whilst the president received regular briefings from Franks as the plan evolved, his questions were not detailed and he offered little in the way of strategic guidance. As Bush put it, 'I have no idea what it takes to cause the Pentagon to respond to a request [to develop a war plan] since I've never been there. I presumed Don Rumsfeld was making sure that the product got done and the process didn't linger.'[33] Of Franks' briefings, Bush later recalled 'the little starbursts' on the planning slides, but not much else.[34] Whereas Rumsfeld was interested in homing in on Franks' assumptions and the precision of his thinking as expressed through the written word, Bush was taking the measure of Franks' demeanour and bearing: 'I'm trying to figure out,' the president told Bob Woodward, 'what questions to ask a commander who has just impressed me in Afghanistan...I'm watching his body language very carefully.'[35] Bush dealt with Franks in the same way he would deal with all his generals until the period of surge decision making: 'Tommy, you are my expert. You've got to tell me what it takes to do it. Anything you need, you'll have.'[36]

Transitioning into Phase IV

Rumsfeld and Franks' military planning focused almost entirely on operations to remove the Saddam regime. Rumsfeld did not see the stabilization of Iraq as something the United States, or at least the Department of Defence, should be involved in. As military expert Frederick Kagan puts it: 'Rumsfeld has a vision of war that is honestly very much like the vision that Moltke had in the nineteenth century. Moltke thought politics stops when the war begins; and starts again when the war ends. The military is not involved before the war, and is not involved after the war. That seems to me to be very much the attitude that Rumsfeld has: when the war's over, it's not his concern anymore.'[37]

Consequently, Franks' war plan contained minimal consideration of transitioning into so-called 'Phase IV' post-hostility operations. Whilst his briefings to

Rumsfeld did consistently include PowerPoint slides on Phase IV, they were often vague and viewed the post-war through the lens of Franks' real concern: Phase III 'kinetic operations'. Thus, the benefit of the speed and precision of Phase III was that little damage would be done to the kind of civilian infrastructure necessary for reconstruction.[38] In practice, this was a false gain: little damage was indeed done to infrastructure during Phase III, but the looting that followed the collapse of the regime eviscerated the country anyway.

Planning was based on the principle that the war would begin with a smaller force, but that reinforcements would flow in behind. Although Franks did not put much effort into detailed Phase IV planning – he knew that he would retire as soon as the regime was defeated – he did signal to the president and to Rumsfeld that Phase IV could take 'years, not months'. The war plan envisaged an in-flow of forces of up to 250,000 over a projected 125 days of fighting. Instead, the fighting was over in 21 days.[39] At the point that US forces entered Baghdad, Rumsfeld stopped the in-flow of reinforcements.[40] Moreover, whereas the plan had called for a major second front from the North, with 4th Infantry Division advancing on Baghdad, the refusal of the Turkish government to grant entry to US forces left the 4th ID floating around at sea on its transports. The rapidity of the fall of the regime, the Turkish refusal to allow US staging of forces, and Rumsfeld's decision to shut off reinforcements meant that actual US troop strength for early stabilization operations was substantially below that envisioned in the war plan.

Almost as soon as Iraqi cities fell to coalition forces, public disorder and looting broke out. The first instances were in the Southern port city of Umm Qasr on 2 April. By the 7th, looting had broken out in the capital. As Baghdad fell, there were only 25,000 US troops to maintain order in a city of 6 million residents.[41]

Some of the looting was random, some systematic. Databases and records of ministries were targeted, both to cover up the misdeeds of the past and to make it more difficult for the Americans to administer the country. The dismantling of heavy machinery –and in some cases, entire factories – bore the hallmarks of an inside job. As Ali Allawi writes, 'In many ministries, individual managers were responsible for organizing and directing the theft and burning of their departments.' Local militias found it a rearmament boon, seizing thousands of tons of weapons from unguarded weapons dumps.[42] The looting elicited perhaps Rumsfeld's most famous comments on the war:

> Stuff happens! But in terms of what's going on in that country, it is a fundamental misunderstanding to see those images over, and over, and over again of some boy walking out with a vase and say, 'oh, my goodness, you didn't have a plan.' That's nonsense. They know what they're doing, and they're doing a terrific job. And it's untidy, and freedom's untidy, and free people are free to make mistakes and commit crimes and do bad things. They're also free to live their lives and do wonderful things, and that's what's going to happen here.[43]

The comment was consistent with Rumsfeld's belief that there is only so much that government action can control. It was a statement of resignation to the will of the mob that echoed many made by philosophical conservatives through the ages. But it was incongruous coming from the deputy Commander in Chief of an occupying military witnessing the disintegration of order in a conquered territory.

Whilst the successes of the invasion plan bore the influence of Rumsfeld's leadership, so did the failure of Phase IV stability operations. As a history manager with a belief in the complexity of the world, Rumsfeld did not believe that direct US action to secure post-Saddam Iraq was wise, and so did not plan extensively for stabilization operations. The president delegated almost all of the planning to Rumsfeld and, by extension, to Franks. Whilst this was congruent with his beliefs on executive management, it led to a dangerous mismatch between his transformational ideas about Iraq and the steps the US would take in service of them.

The story of the immediate aftermath of the invasion is more than a matter of military plans, however. Whilst Rumsfeld was focused upon the war plan, a debate about the proper approach to post-Saddam government was also underway. On this issue, both Bush and Rumsfeld failed, in different ways, to exercise decisive leadership. It would become clear over the coming months and years that whilst Rumsfeld may, de facto, have been the deputy Commander in Chief of an occupying army in Iraq, this was a role that he did not relish.

Notes

1 Bob Woodward, *Plan of Attack* (New York: Simon & Schuster, 2004), 6.
2 Donald H. Rumsfeld, *Known and Unknown* (New York: Sentinel, 2011), 369.
3 Michael R. Gordon and Bernard E. Trainor, *Cobra II: The Inside Story of the Invasion and Occupation of Iraq* (New York: Pantheon Books, 2006), 25.
4 Franks quoted in Peter J. Boyer, 'The New War Machine', *The New Yorker*, 30 June 2003.
5 Gordon and Trainor, *Cobra II*, 22–23.
6 Author interview with Lawrence Di Rita.
7 Woodward, *Plan of Attack*, 35, Rumsfeld, *Known and Unknown*, 439.
8 Woodward, *Plan of Attack*, 34.
9 Rumsfeld, *Known and Unknown*, 429.
10 Woodward, *Plan of Attack*, 32.
11 Woodward, *Plan of Attack*, 1.
12 Boyer, *The New War Machine*.
13 Rumsfeld, *Known and Unknown*, 427.
14 Rumsfeld, *Known and Unknown*, 428.
15 US Department of Defence Notes from Donald Rumsfeld, 'Iraq War Planning', 27 November 2001, available at www.gwu.edu/~nsarchiv/NSAEBB/NSAEBB326/doc08.pdf.
16 Woodward, *Plan of Attack*, 55–56.
17 Woodward, *Plan of Attack*, 62–63.
18 Woodward, *Plan of Attack*, 75–76.

19 Woodward, *Plan of Attack*, 76.
20 Isiah Wilson, 'America's Anabasis', in *War in Iraq: Planning and Execution*, Thomas G. Mahnken and Thomas A. Keaney, eds. (New York: Routledge, 2007), 15–16.
21 Woodward, *Plan of Attack*, 124.
22 Gregory Fontenot, *On Point: The United States Army in Operation Iraqi Freedom* (Annapolis, MD: Naval Institute Press, 2005), 46.
23 Woodward, *Plan of Attack*, 135. A version of the plan as of August 2002 is available online: Central Command, 'Compartmented Concept Update,' 4 August 2002. www.gwu.edu/~nsarchiv/NSAEBB/NSAEBB328/II-Doc16.pdf.
24 Gordon and Trainor, *Cobra II*, 87.
25 Gordon and Trainor, *Cobra II*, 93–94.
26 Boyer, *The New War Machine*.
27 Fontenot, *On Point*, 94.
28 Fontenot, *On Point*, 102.
29 *PBS Frontline*, Interview with Thomas White www.pbs.org/wgbh/pages/frontline/invasion/interviews/white.html.
30 Fontenot, *On Point*, xvii, 74
31 Stephen Biddle, James Emrey, Edward Filiberti, Stephen Kidder, Steven Metz, Ivan Oerlich and Richard Shelton, *Toppling Saddam: Iraq and American Military Transformation* (Carlisle, PA.: Strategic Studies Institute, US Army War College, 2004), 1.
32 John Keegan, *The Iraq War* (New York: Alfred A. Knopf, 2004), 193.
33 Woodward, *Plan of Attack*, 30.
34 Woodward, *Plan of Attack*, 57.
35 Woodward, *Plan of Attack*, 66.
36 Woodward, *Plan of Attack*, 122.
37 *PBS Frontline*, Interview with Frederick Kagan, www.pbs.org/wgbh/pages/frontline/shows/invasion/interviews/kagan.html.
38 Nora Bensahel, Olga Oliker, Keith Crane, Richard R. Brennan, Jr., Heather S. Gregg, Thomas Sullivan, Andrew Rathmell, *After Saddam: Prewar Planning for Postwar Iraq* (Santa Monica, CA: RAND, 2009), 6. Available at www.rand.org/pubs/monographs/MG642/.
39 Mark Fineman, Robin Wright and Doyle McManus, 'Preparing for war, stumbling to peace', *Los Angeles Times*, 18 July 2003.
40 Bensahel et al., *After Saddam*, 15.
41 Special Inspector General for Iraq Reconstruction (SIGIR), *Hard Lessons: The Iraq Reconstruction Experience*, Available at www.sigir.mil/applyinghardlessons/index.html, 82–83.
42 Ali A. Allawi, *The Occupation of Iraq: Winning the War, Losing the Peace* (New Haven, CT: Yale University Press, 2007), 140.
43 Quoted in Thomas E. Ricks, *Fiasco: The American Military Adventure in Iraq* (New York: Penguin, 2006), 136.

5

The governance plan

With the promulgation of the Bush doctrine, the president had been closely engaged whilst the secretary of defence had largely stood aside from policy deliberations. The doctrine bore the clear imprint of the president's worldview. With planning for the invasion of Iraq, Secretary Rumsfeld had taken control, and the president had delegated. The war plan was a Rumsfeld product. Until the surge of December 2006, neither Rumsfeld nor Bush would impose themselves on the course of the war with comparable assertiveness or success.

In this and the following two chapters, we consider Bush and Rumsfeld's decisions over the governance of post-Saddam Iraq, the tenure of the Coalition Provisional Authority (CPA), and the two-year period from the dissolution of CPA until the surge decision. President Bush was committed to creating a democratic Iraq. He felt that it was the responsibility of the United States to create a stable post-Saddam situation so that democracy could take hold. He rejected the notion of exiting Iraq before these goals were achieved. Secretary Rumsfeld was not concerned with creating a democratic regime in Iraq. He did not feel that the US could or should take steps to ensure that. He favoured policies that would minimize US commitment and advance the timetable toward withdrawal, almost regardless of the circumstances that would prevail within Iraq after US forces left.

Remarkably, though, this conflict in approaches was not fully confronted until the period of surge decision making. Rumsfeld, as we saw from the earlier portrait of his style and from the war planning period, did not dictate, but suggested, often elliptically, what he considered to be the right course of action. He would raise questions about the assumptions underpinning the 'stay and democratize' agenda, and would not fully apply his energies and the resources under his control to its achievement. But he did not directly challenge the policies of the president or make his opposition to them clear.

President Bush, committed emotionally and intellectually to the 'stay and democratize' approach, did not engage in a sustained fashion sufficient to uncover the extent of his differences with the secretary of defence. He made decisions when clear options were brought to him, and made interjections into the debate that ensured that Rumsfeld's exit strategy was not implemented. But he did not, until the surge, ascertain the extent of his differences with Rumsfeld. When he did, the president changed both strategy and defence secretary. The conflict between Bush and Rumsfeld was largely subterranean for this long middle period of the administration's Iraq policies. It persisted, unresolved, due to the distinctive combination of Bush and Rumsfeld's executive styles.

In this chapter, I address planning for the political elements of the post-war situation.[1] The issue of what to do about post-Saddam governance should have been of preeminent importance to both Bush and Rumsfeld. It bore directly upon their respective core goals for Iraq. Yet both men gave only intermittent attention to the planning process, and managed the implementation phase so lightly that the independent ideas of their chosen agent in Iraq, Ambassador L. Paul Bremer, became as important to the outcome as those of the president and the secretary of defence.

The United States went to war with a plan to quickly create an 'Iraqi Interim Authority' (IIA) that would be given sovereignty over some areas of Iraqi life immediately and a rolling transfer of authority over others, and that would remove the

Table 5.1 Bush, Rumsfeld and the governance plan

Bush's traits	The governance plan	Rumsfeld's traits	The governance plan
Black-and-white worldview	Fundamental judgement of 'we don't pick Iraq's government'. Surface-level engagement with details on Iraq governance.	Complex worldview	Vacillation on Iraqi Interim Authority policy.
History maker	US should shape Iraqi democracy.	History manager	Believes not possible or proper for US to shape Iraqi post-war politics.
Cheerleading interpersonal style	Unconditional support of Bremer.	Prosecutorial interpersonal style	Difficult, counterproductive relationship with Bremer.
Delegator	Lack of supervision of Bremer. Asked few questions about governance plan and implementation.	Dictator or delegator?	Failed to ensure Bremer was properly briefed, vetted, monitored.

need for the extended period of total US control under what became the CPA. This plan was agreed to in a 10 March National Security Council meeting, and was being implemented during General Jay Garner's period in Iraq. When Garner's replacement, L. Paul Bremer, was selected and briefed, many in the US government believed that he endorsed the IIA plan and would move it to completion. Bremer, however, harboured severe doubts about the wisdom of the concept, and abandoned it within hours of arriving in Iraq. He formalized a direct occupation, putting the CPA in complete control of Iraq's politics and economy for a full year.

The personalities of Bush, who signed off on the IIA but was vague and insouciant with Bremer at a crucial moment, and Rumsfeld, who vacillated on the issue of how much power to give Iraqis in the early stages of the post-war, were crucial as the shape of the new Iraqi politics began to emerge.

Concepts for the post-war

The Bush administration considered three concepts for the governance of post-Saddam Iraq. The fundamental issue differentiating them was the degree and time period of direct US control over Iraqi affairs. Should this control be limited or extensive? Short-term or long-term? Exercised in close collaboration with Iraqis, with the international community, or with neither?[2]

A provisional government

The preference of some officials within the Office of the Secretary of Defence was for declaring an Iraqi provisional government prior to the invasion. This government would be composed of Iraqi exiles and opposition leaders resident in Washington, DC and in London, and based around the Iraqi National Congress organization led by Ahmed Chalabi.

A 'Transitional Civil Authority'

The second concept debated was of an occupation – or, at least, international trusteeship – with Iraq administered by non-Iraqis for an extended period. The strongest advocate of this concept was the State Department, which developed an outline plan for a Transitional Civil Authority (TCA).[3] Such an authority would hopefully gain a mandate from the United Nations and could provide strong central leadership for a 'multi-year transitional period' in order to 'build democratic institutions'.[4] During the period of direct rule, exiles would return to the country and establish political parties and movements that would compete with, or be absorbed by, similar parties formed by in-country Iraqis. Some of the dangers of a provisional government – empowering untrustworthy exiles and instantly turning over control of a country without the foundations of democracy – would be avoided. Additionally, the full resources, expertise and legitimacy of the international community could be brought to bear.

The MacArthur Model

The third possibility was for direct rule by those who had overthrown the regime – the US military. CENTCOM Commander Gen. Tommy Franks could act as a unified source of civil and military authority, ruling by decree. The obvious analogy here was to the period of post-1945 occupation of Japan and the level of control exercised by Gen. Douglas MacArthur. The Joint Staff proposed this in autumn 2002, calling for a 'three-star general in charge of a staff of experts drawn from various US government agencies.'[5]

Decision and indecision by Bush and Rumsfeld

After several months of debate, and with the start date for the war approaching, these three concepts emerged from the tertiary and secondary levels of the interagency process and were considered by the full National Security Council.

The principals reached two conclusions. First, the idea of declaring a provisional government in exile was dismissed. Rumsfeld, characteristically, saw the issue as complex. He distrusted the exiles, but was attracted to the opportunity they offered to minimize US post-war involvement. His interventions on the issue were inconsistent. Under-secretary for Policy Douglas Feith discussed the idea with the secretary:

> Rumsfeld said the problem is that if you simply have a provisional government, even if you get the internals involved in it quickly, you would be putting an enormous amount of power and enormous resources, economic and military, in the hands of these people, and they may not prove themselves competent, they may not prove themselves honest, and they may not prove themselves politically successful. So he said the provisional government idea is not a good idea. Even though we had done something like a provisional government in Afghanistan, Rumsfeld said the difference between Iraq and Afghanistan is that Afghanistan didn't have the economic resources or the military resources that Iraq had.[6]

Most importantly, the president himself disliked the idea of declaring in advance a government for liberated Iraq, believing it to be inconsistent with his goal of bringing democracy to the country. When Chalabi's name was mentioned in early 2003 National Security Council meetings by Feith and Wolfowitz, the president said that 'this is about democracy... we're not putting our thumb on the scale.'[7] Bush's commitment to democratization was more than mere rhetoric.

The second decision reached by the principals was that the Department of Defence would be the lead agency in the post-war – a move that made the Bush/Rumsfeld conflict even more crucial to US policy in Iraq. The logic in favour of Pentagon control was compelling. The Pentagon had the necessary resources and since executing policy involved issuing orders to military personnel, the secretary of defence had to be in charge. Even Powell agreed: 'State does not have the personnel, the capacity, or the size to deal with an immediate post-war situation in a foreign country that's eight thousand miles away from here.'[8] The decision was formalized in National Security Presidential Directive (NSPD-24).

Decision making was less crisp in terms of deciding upon the fundamental concept for post-war governance. As Rumsfeld later described it,

> In discussions of post-war Iraq, the toughest challenge was the tension between two different strategic approaches. The debate between them was legitimate, but it remained just that – a debate. It was never hashed out at the NSC and never finally resolved…the basic difference was between speed – how quickly we could turn over authority – and what was called legitimacy – exactly what political and constitutional processes needed to be in place prior to turning the reins over.[9]

Both Bush and Rumsfeld experienced internal conflict on the issue. The president was at the beginning of an intellectual journal on questions of stability and governance in post-conflict states. Bush had campaigned on a foreign policy platform of 'no nation-building', arguing that the 'armed social work' of the 1990s was an inappropriate use of US military resources. But the president had become emotionally and intellectually committed to democratization – an ambitious goal that required a great degree of nation-building.[10] Had 'no nation-building' been Bush's sole objective, he would have supported the provisional government in exile concept. But with 'no nation-building' competing with 'democratization' as a goal, the risk was in desiring the creation of democratic institutions without fully committing to the 'armed social work' necessary to achieve them. As Marc Grossman reports, 'although people were fighting about this tactic and that tactic, part of the issue was there were these unresolved philosophical debates about nation-building.'[11]

Rumsfeld was also conflicted. The secretary did not want a period of US occupation of Iraq. This ran counter to his more technology/less manpower model for the US armed forces. At the same time, as noted above, Rumsfeld had doubts about anointing a group of exiles as the government of a country with the wealth and resources of Iraq. Lawrence Di Rita and Douglas Feith both confirm that Rumsfeld's decision making on this issue was driven by a conflict between his belief that nation-building is not an appropriate action for US armed forces and his desire to make sure that the post-Hussein leadership was effective.

Moreover, the top decision makers were managing several other issues. Their time was short and their attention often elsewhere. The president was heavily consumed with the diplomatic effort to secure United Nations support for the war. Secretary Rumsfeld's prime concern was with the in-depth process of 'iterated planning' on the invasion plan. As he said apologetically to Jay Garner on 14 March, 'I haven't given you the time I should have given you. Quite frankly, I just have been so engulfed in the war that I just didn't have time to focus on everything that you're doing. I tried to keep abreast of it, but I wasn't able to give it the time it needed.'[12]

The result was that official policy for post-war governance, as decided by the principals, remained vague until very late in the process.[13] A short NSC document, 'Iraq: Goals, Objectives, Strategies', represented the codified position. The document spoke of 'an interim administration in Iraq that prepares for the transition to an elected Iraqi government as quickly as practicable.'[14] Of course, without further specification, this interim administration could fit with any of the concepts discussed above. And the timetable of 'as quickly as practicable' was similarly imprecise.

a compromise solution

The Iraqi Interim Authority concept and the 10 March National Security Council meeting

A decision on the form of post-war governance in Iraq was not made until 10 March 2003, just days before the invasion of Iraq. Once the president had decided against declaring a provisional government in exile, Douglas Feith had gone to work on a compromise.[15] His proposal was an Iraqi Interim Authority that would share power with the coalition. This Authority would immediately have power over some areas of governance, such as the ministries of foreign affairs, justice and agriculture. As the IIA broadened in representation, proved its competence and the situation stabilized, it would take control over more and more ministries until, in a relatively short period of time, it assumed control over the 'power ministries' and became a fully fledged sovereign government.[16]

As Feith explained, it was designed to take the best elements of the TCA and provisional government concepts, whilst avoiding the risks of both:

> It wasn't an all or nothing: it wasn't we run the whole country, as State had said, and it wasn't we turn everything over immediately, as the provisional government idea had said. This was: you [the Iraqis] will have a sovereign government from the beginning, or nearly the beginning, but you will not be totally sovereign in all areas right away. Instead, we will have a power sharing arrangement, and we will be transferring increasing amounts of authority to you as soon as we can and as soon as we satisfy ourselves that you are functioning well and honestly and with popular support.[17]

The concept was discussed in two preparatory NSC meetings on 1 and 7 March, and agreed to in an NSC meeting on 10 March.[18]

Enter Jay Garner

With the decision on post-war structure seemingly made, attention turned to implementation. Retired Lieutenant General Jay Garner was recruited and placed in charge of a new team: the Organization for Reconstruction and Humanitarian Assistance (ORHA). Garner was charged with integrating the planning that had been done by various interagency groups, and shaping ORHA into a unit that could deal with immediate post-war humanitarian needs and get together a nascent Iraqi Interim Authority.

Garner begins to implement the IIA plan

Rumsfeld wrote to the president and the other principals on 1 April indicating the importance of moving forward with the IIA: 'We have to get moving on this ... This is now a matter of operational importance. It is not too much to say that time can cost lives.'[19] With a similar sense of urgency, Garner began to aggressively implement the IIA plan upon arrival in Baghdad. He met with an anxious Ahmad Chalabi on the night of 14 April, in the Southern city of Nasiriyah. Chalabi wanted to be transported to Baghdad as quickly as possible in order to prevent the emergence of a post-Saddam governance vacuum.[20]

On 28 April, Garner met with prominent Iraqi leaders in Baghdad. This meeting advanced the IIA concept substantially, and was characterized by a new spirit of cooperation among the previously fractious Iraqi leaders. A timetable for the establishment of a transitional government was established, with agreement to hold a conference in northern Iraq within a month to determine its membership and leadership mechanisms – president, prime minister or executive council.[21] A week later, Garner, brimming with optimism, held a press conference:

> Five opposition leaders have begun having meetings and are going to bring in leaders from the inside of Iraq and see if that can't form a nucleus of leadership as we enter into June ... Next week, or by the second weekend in May, you'll see the beginning of a nucleus of a temporary Iraqi government, a government with an Iraqi face on it that is totally dealing with the coalition.[22]

Enter Jerry Bremer

US actions had, to this point, been consistent with the decision to create an Iraqi Interim Authority. Once Jay Garner was replaced by Paul Bremer, the IIA policy was abandoned. Bush's delegatory style, his bolstering approach to interpersonal relations and Rumsfeld's vacillation on a complex issue are central to an understanding of how this happened.

Contrary to later reports that Garner was fired as the situation spiralled out of control, it had always been the intention to replace Garner with a diplomat once the IIA process was established. The timeline for deploying Garner's replacement was brought forward, but this was a measure of the success Garner had had in his contacts with Iraqi leaders. Lawrence Di Rita, seconded from Rumsfeld's staff to ORHA to serve as a policy advisor, said 'it was happening fast. And so if the politics was coming together, we had to get the politics team out there...The IIA was coming together, we had the conferences, and there was the clear desire by the Iraqis to get us out of the way, or at least have us play our proper role.'[23]

Several options were considered for Garner's replacement. Deputy Secretary of Defence Paul Wolfowitz even suggested himself. In early May 2003, Ambassador L. Paul Bremer was contacted. Bremer had over 20 years' experience in the State Department, serving in special assistant or executive assistant positions for six Secretaries of State. During the 1980s he had been Ambassador to the Netherlands, and then Ambassador at Large for Counter-Terrorism. He then worked out of government at Henry Kissinger's consulting firm, and at the time he was contacted he was chairman and CEO of Marsh Crisis Consulting.[24]

Bremer, by his own admission an expert in neither Iraqi politics and society or post-war reconstruction generally, turned out to have strong views on both. Bush and Rumsfeld's uneven management of him, and Rumsfeld's vacillation as regards post-war governance, would give Bremer great leeway to pursue his ideas once he was out in Iraq. Perhaps as a result of his State Department career, Bremer was leery of handing over power to the Iraqis too soon and keen to establish a comprehensive constitutional and political structure, along with full elections, before doing so. He forwarded to Rumsfeld a study on post-1945 reconstruction efforts involving the US and wrote in a covering note that he viewed one of the key lessons as '[s]taying a long time does not guarantee success. Leaving early assures failure.' Bremer highlighted a line in the study that stressed 'No effort at democratization has taken hold in less than five years.'[25] When he heard on his car radio that Garner expected an Iraqi Interim Authority to be ready to go by 15 May, he 'almost drove off the George Washington Parkway'. Bremer reports believing that 'it would take careful work to disabuse both the Iraqi and American proponents of this reckless fantasy'.[26]

US policy now became dangerously ambiguous, and neither Bush nor Rumsfeld took effective action to clarify it. Bremer did not seek clarification of the IIA concept or ask for a reconsideration of it. Instead, he talked directly to the president in a one-on-one lunch on 6 May. Bremer said to the president that it would take time for Iraq to attain a 'stable political structure'.[27] According to Bremer, Bush responded that he was 'fully committed to bringing representative government to Iraq...we'll stay until the job is done'. Further, Bremer said he should be able to exercise broad authority in responding to what would be a very fluid situation. Bush agreed, and told Bremer to 'get over there, and give us your recommendations'.[28]

After the lunch, the president ushered Bremer into a meeting with the principals, saying 'I don't know whether we need this meeting after all. Jerry and I have just had it.' This was music to the Ambassador's ears: 'His message was clear. I was neither Rumsfeld's man nor Powell's man. I was the president's man.'[29] Bremer took these presidential remarks – clubbable, insouciant and vague – as indicating that the IIA was no longer set policy, but instead one option that he could choose to follow once he got to Iraq, based upon his personal reading of the situation.

Bremer created not an Iraqi Interim Authority but an 'Iraqi Governing Council' (IGC). The name was grand, but the role was circumscribed. The IGC would have a strictly limited advisory standing. To govern the country, Bremer, as we will see in the next chapter, turned the Coalition Provisional Authority into a full-blown executive/administrative body, ruling by decree over all aspects of civil governance. He began playing the part of MacArthur in Japan: 'My new assignment did combine some of the vice regal responsibilities of […] MacArthur' he told an aide, but 'I'd settle for MacArthur's problems. Conditions weren't this complicated for him.'[30]

Bremer claims he received clear discretionary authority direct from the Commander in Chief: 'the president's instructions to me…when I had lunch with him alone on May 6th, were that we were going to take our time to get it right… The president had effectively, though perhaps not formally, changed his position on the question of a short or long occupation, having before the war been in favor of a short occupation. By the time I came in, that was gone.'[31]

He believes that in the 8 May principals committee meeting following that lunch, he received cabinet authorization for his approach. According to Bremer's memoir, the president said an Iraqi government was '*not* going to happen overnight, despite what exile leaders hope or even believe'; Powell told him to 'get a representative group…We should let Iraqi leaders emerge'; the vice president said 'We need a strategy on the ground for the post-war situation we actually have and not the one we wish we had'.[32] At the same meeting Rumsfeld, displaying his habit of seeing both sides of the argument to a chronic degree, expressed his view that it would be a mistake to anoint the exiles.[33]

Readers of Bremer's memoir are struck with the Ambassador's determination to, in his words, put on his 'desert boots…to start kicking some butt'.[34] The analogies foremost in his mind are those of the occupations of Germany and Japan.[35] Rumsfeld read these sections of the memoir with interest: 'I had no idea that he would see himself this way. It certainly was not a mindset that was conducive to working with proud and wary Iraqis or with the large American military contingent in the country.'[36]

The puzzle concerning post-war governance in Iraq is not, as is commonly stated, why there was no post-war planning. As Feith says, there was little planning for the problems that arose during the CPA occupation, because 'we weren't planning to run an occupation'.[37] Instead, the question is why did the United States government fail to implement the planning it had conducted and, specifically, bring into being the Iraqi Interim Authority on which the president had been briefed and which he had endorsed? The Bush/Rumsfeld styles are again at the core of the explanation.

Bush had the authority to decide and insist upon any plan he wished. His conflicting beliefs – no nation-building combined with a commitment to the democratization of Iraq – did not offer a clear roadmap as concepts were presented to him. At a crucial moment, his approach to interpersonal relations with L. Paul Bremer – seeking to bolster Bremer's confidence and feeling of importance at the critical 8 May lunch – gave Bremer a sense of having the Commander in Chief's backing to essentially decide the policy on his own once he arrived in Iraq. Bush's clubbable nature and desire to bolster the morale of subordinates at the expense, on occasion, of issuing them with detailed instructions, was crucial. Lawrence Di Rita explained:

> My impression is that Jerry relied on his personal relationship with the President, and I don't doubt the president said the things the Jerry says that he says: use your best judgment and those sorts of things. The history of foreign policy is written in part by those sorts of communications, so it's not shocking to me that a President's communication to an envoy, that envoy would see as guidance. But I doubt that the President would have intended that by virtue of a comment he was undoing policy decisions that had been taken by the apparatus of the government. But that appears to be what happened. In other words, we spent a lot of time - we the government - creating the IIA process, it's documented and promulgated through a written directive of the President. That's how things are supposed to work. Presidents shouldn't be placed in the position of being seen as giving separate guidance outside of the interagency process.[38]

Bush may not have intended that, but the episode highlights the potential dangers of his approach to interpersonal relations and his tendency to avoid persistent, detailed engagement with policy.

Rumsfeld recorded his uneasiness the day of the Bush/Bremer lunch in a handwritten note: 'POTUS had lunch with him [Bremer] alone. Shouldn't have done so. POTUS linked him to the White House instead of DoD [Department of Defense] or DoS [Department of State].'[39] As Rumsfeld put it in his memoirs 'Bush, at least in my presence, never wavered in his desire to turn power over to the Iraqis as quickly as possible. Then again, he never firmly resisted the State Department's efforts to slow the timeline either. This ambiguity may have been just enough for Bremer to decide he had Bush's support for delay.'[40] The president's delegatory nature and dislike of detailed engagement led to his failure to clarify the ambiguities between the IIA concept and Bremer's interpretation of his instructions.

Rumsfeld's worldview and management style were also important here. As with the president, the secretary of defence held contradictory beliefs about the issue of post-war governance. He abhorred nation-building, but was uneasy about setting up a provisional government of exiles. Rumsfeld refused to give the Deputies Committee authority to decide and implement policy, reserving decisions for the principals. However, when the decision was addressed at the cabinet level,

he vacillated on the issue of a quick transfer of sovereignty, with his most sceptical contributions to the idea coming at precisely the point that Bremer was being
briefed that a quick transfer was US policy. Soon after Bremer begun work in Iraq,
Rumsfeld returned to advocating a rapid transition.[41] Although Rumsfeld's memoir
presents him as being consistently and decisively in favour of a rapid transition,
he was less than constant on the issue.[42] Rumsfeld himself acknowledges that his
style caused difficulties in this instance: 'Contrary to popular perception, I was not
inclined to issue direct, detailed, not to be questioned orders to those who work for
me. I have found that people at senior levels generally do better when given broad
guidelines and the leeway to exercise their judgment as changing circumstances
arise. In Bremer's case, he had too much leeway.'[43]

Notes

1 An expanded version of the argument in this chapter, focused more on the role of L. Paul
   Bremer and the details of the planning process, can be found in Stephen Benedict Dyson,
   'What Really Happened in Planning for Postwar Iraq?', *Political Science Quarterly*.
2 See Special Inspector General for Iraq Reconstruction, *Hard Lessons: The Iraq Reconstruction
   Experience*, 6, for a similar discussion of the conceptual options. Available at www.sigir.mil/
   applyinghardlessons/index.html.
3 Douglas J. Feith, 'Comments on State Papers', 28 July 2002. Available at www.waranddeci-
   sion.com/docLib/20080422_CommentonStatepapers.pdf.
4 SIGIR, *Hard Lessons*, 7.
5 Bradley Graham, *By His Own Rules: The Ambitions, Successes, and Ultimate Failures of Donald
   Rumsfeld* (New York: Public Affairs, 2009), 378.
6 Author interview with Feith.
7 Fred Kaplan, *Daydream Believers: How a Few Grand Ideas Wrecked American Power* (New
   York: Wiley, 2008), 155. See also Bush, *Decision Points*, 249.
8 SIGIR, *Hard Lessons*, 49.
9 Donald H. Rumsfeld, *Known and Unknown* (New York: Sentinel, 2011), 486.
10 Elizabeth N. Saunders, *Leaders at War* (Ithaca, NY: Cornell University Press, 2011),
   198–205.
11 Author interview with Marc A. Grossman.
12 Bob Woodward, *State of Denial: Bush at War Part III* (New York: Simon & Schuster, 2007),
   149–150.
13 Rumsfeld, *Known and Unknown*, 485.
14 Condoleezza Rice, 'Iraq: Goals, Objectives, Strategy', NSC memo, 29 October 2002.
   Available at www.waranddecision.com/docLib/20080402_IraqGoalsStrategy.pdf; see also
   SIGIR, *Hard Lessons*, 13.
15 On the compromise nature of the IIA proposal, see Feith's handwritten note on Peter
   Rodman's paper proposing essentially a provisional government and arguing against State's
   proposal: 'Worth reading. Though I don't think Peter's recommendations are necessarily
   inconsistent with creating a US-led Transitional Civil Authority.' Available at http://library.
   Rumsfeld.com/doclib/sp/313/2002-08-15%20from%20Peter%20Rodman%20re%20
   Who%20Will%20Govern%20Iraq.pdf.

16 James Dobbins, *Occupying Iraq: A History of the Coalition Provisional Authority* (Santa Monica, CA: RAND Corporation, 2009), 38. Available at www.rand.org/pubs/monographs/2009/RAND_MG847.pdf.

17 Author interview with Feith.

18 SIGIR, *Hard Lessons*, 62; Feith, *War and Decision*, 405; Rumsfeld, *Known and Unknown*, 491.

19 Secretary Rumsfeld to President Bush, 'Iraqi Interim Authority', 4 January 2003, available at http://library.Rumsfeld.com/doclib/sp/321/2003-04-01%20to%20President%20Bush%20re%20Iraqi%20Interim%20Authority.pdf.

20 *PBS Frontline* interview with Garner.

21 Rajiv Chandresekaran and Monte Reel, 'Iraqis Set Timetable to Take Power', *Washington Post*, 29 April 2003; see also Karen DeYoung and Glenn Kessler, 'US to Seek Iraqi Interim Authority', *Washington Post*, 24 April 2003; Douglas Jehl and Eric Schmitt, 'US Reported to Push for Iraqi Government, with Pentagon Prevailing', *New York Times*, 30 April 2003.

22 Patrick E. Tyler, 'Opposition Groups to Help Create Assembly in Iraq', *New York Times*, 6 May 2003.

23 Author interview with Di Rita.

24 Dobbins, *Occupying Iraq*, 11.

25 Ambassador Bremer to Secretary Rumsfeld, 'Nation Building: Lessons Learned', 4 May 2003. Available at http://library.Rumsfeld.com/doclib/sp/418/From%20Ambassador%20Bremer%20re%20Nation-Building,%20Lessons%20Learned%20with%20Attachment%2005-04-2003.pdf.

26 L. Paul Bremer, *My Year in Iraq: The Struggle to Build a Future of Hope* (New York: Simon & Schuster, 2006), 12.

27 Bremer, *My Year in Iraq*, 12.

28 *PBS Frontline* Interview with L. Paul Bremer, 26 June and 18 August 2006, available at www.pbs.org/wgbh/pages/frontline/yeariniraq/interviews/bremer.html.

29 Bremer, *My Year in Iraq*, 12.

30 Bremer, *My Year in Iraq*, 37.

31 SIGIR, *Hard Lessons*, 69.

32 Bremer, *My Year in Iraq*, 43.

33 Bremer, *My Year in Iraq*, 42–43.

34 Bremer, *My Year in Iraq*, 29.

35 Bremer, *My Year in Iraq*, 19; 37.

36 Rumsfeld, *Known and Unknown*, 508.

37 Author interview with Feith.

38 Author interview with Di Rita.

39 Rumsfeld, *Known and Unknown*, 506.

40 Rumsfeld, *Known and Unknown*, 510.

41 Donald Rumsfeld to Paul Bremer, 'Why we need an IA sooner rather than later', 9 June 2003. Available at http://library.Rumsfeld.com/doclib/sp/334/2003-06-09%20to%20Paul%20Bremer%20re%20Why%20We%20Need%20an%20IA%20Sooner%20Rather%20Than%20Later.pdf.

42 Dan Senor and Roman Martinez, 'Rumsfeld's Iraq Revisionism', *Washington Post*, 15 February 2011, p. A21.

43 Rumsfeld, *Known and Unknown*, 512.

6

Coalition Provisional Authority

With the Iraqi Interim Authority concept abandoned, Bush and Rumsfeld allowed the Coalition Provisional Authority (CPA) to become an instrument of occupation. The CPA was characterized by confusion over objectives and organization of a kind that Rumsfeld usually found intolerable. It had an ambiguous mandate, an odd relationship with the military, and multiple lines of reporting back to Washington, DC. This led to the confusion that the secretary usually considered to be the result of faulty underlying assumptions. CPA was also profoundly under-resourced. Bush should have recognized and rectified this as CPA was the instrument for shaping post-war Iraqi politics, but his delegatory style was apparent once more.

The mission of the CPA changed several times over the course of its tenure. Initially meant to be a short-duration partner to an Iraqi Interim Authority, it morphed into a full-scale occupation authority with plans to oversee a multi-year process of constitution writing and government building, only to remake itself again in summer 2004 into a transitional authority handing off to a new Iraqi government.

Its staffing levels were in constant flux. It sought to set security policy and train an Iraqi police force, then had to abandon both efforts. In every way, then, CPA was the type of organizational nightmare that Rumsfeld should have found unacceptable. Yet Rumsfeld allowed the situation to occur and to persist. He did not want to micro-manage CPA, and was averse to having the Defence Department involved in post-conflict activities. As he put it in his memoirs, 'Though I would have entered Iraq with a different mindset had I been in [CPA Administrator] Bremer's shoes, I wasn't in his shoes.'[1]

Bush liked Bremer and sought to give him uncritical backing. The president believed he had given Bremer clear instructions, and his proper role now, he thought, was to allow Bremer to execute them. In this chapter, I trace the impact of Bush and Rumsfeld on this period of policy in Iraq, arguing that the confusion and counter-productive elements of CPA behaviour were conditioned by the styles of these two leaders.

Table 6.1 Coalition Provisional Authority (CPA)

Bush's traits	The post-war	Rumsfeld's traits	The post-war
Black-and-white worldview	Surface-level engagement with details on CPA, army, constitution. Absolute commitment to holding elections. 'Bring 'em on' approach to insurgency.	Complex worldview	Vacillation on timing of hand-off to Iraqis. Rejection of 'insurgency' label.
History maker	Commitment to democratization of Iraq and Freedom Agenda. Commitment to defeating insurgency.	History manager	Believes CPA should not try to oversee new Iraqi political system. Believes insurgency cannot be defeated by US forces at acceptable cost.
Cheerleading interpersonal style	Continued support of Bremer.	Prosecutorial interpersonal style	Continued difficult relationship with Bremer.
Delegator	Continued light supervision of Bremer. Lack of engagement with Rumsfeld's different approach to CPA strategy.	Dictator or delegator?	Inconsistent approach to Bremer, tries to hand-off responsibility for managing him. Micromanaging CPA personnel requests whilst allowing overall CPA mission to drift.

Coalition Provisional Authority – a confused chain of command

Rumsfeld sent Bremer a letter of appointment instructing him to 'oversee, direct and coordinate all executive, legislative and judicial functions' in Iraq 'including humanitarian relief and reconstruction'.[2] The CPA also received a mandate from the United Nations. On 22 May, the UN passed resolution 1483 naming the

US and UK as occupying powers of Iraq, with the consequent responsibility to name and support a government of occupation. This was a departure from other interventions of the modern era, which the UN had sanctioned as peacekeeping missions.[3]

CPA, then, was a creation of the US government, the executive authority of a foreign country, and had an explicit mandate from the United Nations. This made it difficult to understand precisely what CPA's status was – a US government agency, a mission of the United Nations, the trustee administration of Iraq, or all of the above? Bremer himself was a presidential representative, but his orders were to report directly to the secretary of defence. As a presidential representative, Bremer felt he could contact and report to Bush directly or through the National Security Council staff, and of course the president had been very warm toward him in their informal interactions. However, the Department of Defence retained the authority of NSPD-24, putting the Pentagon in charge of post-war activities, and Bremer's memo of appointment instructed him to report to Rumsfeld. Compounding the confusion, Bremer was a veteran of the State Department, and had been appointed precisely to fulfil more ambassadorial duties than the operationally minded Jay Garner. So he had a right and responsibility to report to the White House and the Pentagon, and had strong career ties to the State Department.

However, Bremer was also the top authority in a foreign country, a status endorsed by UN resolution. The CPA assumed control over Iraqi assets, and impounded monies under the oil-for-food programme. That was clearly Iraqi money. Bremer himself felt that 'it is not entirely clear that the CPA was a US government entity', while his closest aide, Ambassador Clay McManaway, believed that 'CPA was the Iraqi government; it was not an American entity…Jerry Bremer was the custodian of the Iraqi people'.[4]

If there was confusion over the nature of CPA and Bremer's reporting relationships – and the real importance of this was to blur the question of who could give orders to the CPA head – the tangle was only tighter when it came to relations with coalition military forces in Iraq. If Bremer was the top authority in the country and reported directly to the secretary of defence, it followed that he had a claim to control the levers of force. General Sanchez later wrote that Bremer believed the military should do what he said. In his memoirs, Bremer writes that it was customary for someone of ambassadorial rank (which was the least he believed he held) to be treated by the in-country military commander as a three-star general – i.e., Sanchez's equal. He did not seek to issue operational orders, but did feel that the military should act upon his strategic plans. US generals are used to taking orders from civilian commanders in chief, but not from a US ambassador in the field. Sanchez felt this would have been 'civilian *command* of the military, and that was not acceptable'.[5] The military ignored Bremer when his wishes seemed to them to be unwise.

Organization and staffing

In multiple ways, then, CPA had confusing lines of authority, and Bush did not act to clarify them. CPA also had staffing problems, and Rumsfeld, who did not believe in the ends CPA was pursuing, did not provide the means to achieve them. Bremer complained constantly about CPA staffing. In order to provide staff, Rumsfeld's Pentagon engaged in a rushed and unconventional search process in Washington, DC, recruiting from the youthful-ranks of the email listservs of right-leaning think tanks. The difficulty was that these enthusiastic individuals were rarely experts in regional matters or in the substantive roles they were given. They also tended to be male, in a ratio of 10–1, creating a somewhat charged workplace atmosphere. In addition to lacking experience, these young staffers remained in Iraq for an average of three months – just long enough to begin to understand their jobs – before returning to the US.

Bremer raised the issue of staffing on many occasions with Rumsfeld, but did so in a way that, given Rumsfeld's temperament, was counter-productive. A consistent feature of Rumsfeld's mode of operation was to be careful with manpower. As with his approach to the planning of the invasion itself, he was sceptical of requests for additional numbers of people, believing that they were often ill-founded and wasteful. With his belief in precision and paperwork, Rumsfeld insisted that any manpower request be meticulously documented and justified.

In the early months of CPA, however, Bremer had little idea how many people were working for him. He just knew that the number was not high enough. Bremer's top aides recall that people simply arrived and then left again without much tracking of the comings and goings. His close aide Ambassador Clayton McManaway notes that 'we needed to formalize a way for people to get into – and out of – Iraq. But we didn't even have the capability to send a cable when we arrived.' Rumsfeld found it ludicrous to receive a request for more staff from an organization that could not keep track of the manpower it already had, and so did not make the issue a priority.[6] As with other manifestations of this part of Rumsfeld's belief system – the issue of troop numbers being the most oft-cited – it made good sense from a corporate efficiency standpoint, but was problematic in the inherently wasteful environment of war.

Rumsfeld felt that the fundamental problem was that Bremer and the CPA were performing tasks that had not been planned for. 'Bremer's ambitions went far beyond the limited role for the United States that the Department of Defense and the interagency process had planned for and well beyond the role that had been resourced…The means were not well linked to the ends.'[7] Rumsfeld did not believe in the ends, and so did not exert effort to expand the means. The president, who did believe in the ends, failed to notice the mismatch between the ambitious goals for Iraq that Bremer articulated and the resources at Bremer's disposal. The president liked what he heard from Bremer about taking charge of the situation and building a new Iraq, but did not get into the detail of how this would come to pass.

Disbanding the Iraqi Army

On 12 March 2003, the National Security Council (NSC) discussed what to do with the Iraqi army once the Saddam regime was removed. They decided to keep the army in being to use in policing or reconstruction operations. On 22 May 2003, Bremer, on a secure videoconference line from Baghdad, announced that he intended to issue a directive disbanding the army. This was a critical change in policy, and had lasting consequences. Was it cleared with Bush, Rumsfeld and the other principals, or was it freelancing by Bremer?[8] Bush and Rumsfeld's leadership styles are again at the centre of the controversy.

In considering what to do with the Iraqi army prior to the war, officials in the Office of the Secretary of Defence (OSD) had liaised with Jay Garner and the leadership of the newly constituted Organization for Reconstruction and Humanitarian Affairs (ORHA). Garner wanted to make use of the manpower available within the ranks of the Iraqi army.[9] OSD briefing slides from January 2003 indicate that there was a nuanced discussion of the issue. Much depended on the circumstances following the conflict. If the Iraqi army leadership played a 'positive role' in ending the conflict, 'US emphasis would be on reforming' the army rather than disbanding it. If, however, there were mass desertions, 'US emphasis might be on creating a new army'.[10]

In the 12 March 2003 NSC meeting, Douglas Feith led the briefing. The idea, he said, was to disband the part of the army that was loyal to Saddam, to retain three to five well-trained divisions to form the core of a new army, and to utilize most of the conscript remainder on an ad hoc basis as general labour. The rationale was that Iraq's army was highly stratified – only a small portion at the top were Baathists, a second level was quite well trained, but the mass had been dragooned into service and were mediocre soldiers. Offer them a small salary and you would have the advantage of some manpower, whilst avoiding the danger of making hundreds of thousands of armed young men redundant. To Feith, keeping the Iraqi army had both upsides and downsides. The labour would be useful, but this was still an instrument of the Saddamist state. It was a close call, but the balance of advantage lay with retaining the army.[11] The president accepted the recommendations without much comment, as he had the policy of standing up an Iraqi Interim Authority. Bush's tendency to accept a recommendation without investigating the underlying rationale could leave him unable to understand the significance of changes in policy – as happened with both the IIA and the question of the Iraqi army.

Bremer had not been selected as head of the new Coalition Provisional Authority by the time of this decision. After he was hired, he once again proved to have strong views on a previously decided issue. Bremer was keen to establish a theme for his arrival in Baghdad: 'The Baathists are not coming back'. Along with a decree announcing a programme of De-Baathification, an order disbanding the army would dramatize his arrival.

The core of the controversy is how much Bremer developed the disbandment order with officials from OSD and cleared it with Rumsfeld, versus how much it was a surprise to all, including the secretary of defence and the president, when he appeared on a satellite video-link and announced a fait accompli.

Bremer's view is that the decision to disband was made in full consultation with Paul Wolfowitz and Douglas Feith, that Rumsfeld and Bush were told it was coming, and that no objections were raised at any stage. Moreover, the decision was obviously correct, Bremer believes, as the Iraqi army had effectively self-demobilized.[12] Feith confirms that Bremer and Slocombe did discuss dissolution with him, and that he supported their judgement given that much of the army had gone home. '[M]any of the key reasons to *preserve* the army no longer applied, while the arguments for *dissolving* it were still relevant.'[13]

Bremer suggests that CENTCOM commander General John Abizaid pronounced in mid-April 2003 that the Iraqi army had ceased to exist, whilst Rumsfeld gave the CPA head a briefing document indicating that a core objective was to 'eliminate the remnants of Saddam's regime' – including the army. In early May, Bremer asserts that he worked out the details of a disbandment order in consultation with Wolfowitz and Feith. By 9 May, the order was complete, and Bremer sent it for clearance to Rumsfeld, Wolfowitz, Feith and Tommy Franks, amongst others. A final version was circulated on 19 May, and Bremer says he received detailed comments from top officials in OSD and US military leaders in Iraq, indicating that the document was read and understood.[14]

Bremer then sent Bush a letter on 22 May reporting on his initial activities in Iraq. The central issue, he wrote, was convincing Iraqis that Saddam's regime was not coming back. In this context, his dissolution of the Baath party had been well – even joyously – received, and he was now going to promulgate an 'even more robust measure dissolving Saddam's military and intelligence structures'.[15] Bush responded positively and without raising any objections. 'Your leadership is apparent,' Bush wrote. 'You have quickly made a positive and significant impact. You have my full support and confidence.'[16] It seemed, certainly to Bremer, that Bush was not inclined to enquire much into the details of what the ambassador was doing. This impression was reinforced by an interview the president gave to his biographer Robert Draper, where he seemed to have given the matter little further consideration: 'The policy was to keep the army intact. Didn't happen.'[17]

Rumsfeld does not seem to have thought deeply about the decision at the time, although he did look into it later and had his aide Peter Rodman reconstruct the process in a memo.[18] Bob Woodward asked Rumsfeld whether Bremer cleared the disbandment order with Pentagon leadership. '[I]t would be a surprise to me' Rumsfeld said, 'if Wolfowitz and Feith gave him those orders. I just don't know that.' Did Rumsfeld know the disbandment order was coming? 'I can't say I did. I simply don't recall it, and I don't recall an NSC meeting on the subject, but that doesn't mean there wasn't one. That's just my best recollection today.'[19] Rumsfeld was more forthright in his memoirs: 'I was told of Bremer's decision and possibly could have stopped it.'[20]

Frank Miller, senior director for Iraq on the National Security Council staff, believes that Bremer performed a deliberate end-run around the normal policy-making system.

> [It] was a deliberate subversion of the interagency process. The decision made by the president on March 12, 2003 was that we will keep the Iraqi army intact. I know because it was my briefing, I briefed it to the deputies, and I briefed it to the principals twice. At the second briefing Rumsfeld said to me 'you're not briefing on the Iraqi army – that's a DOD matter.' So Doug Feith presented my brief to the President and the NSC on March 12. Subsequently Bremer goes out to Iraq, sends some sort of warning to Feith and Rumsfeld, neither of whom tell the other senior interagency participants, and there is a video conference and Bremer says to the president 'I am about to sign a decree abolishing the army.' No warning, no knowledge, no one in the room that knows anything about it except Feith and Rumsfeld. And so there is this moment of stunned silence, then the president says 'you're the guy on the ground Jerry, you make the call.'[21]

Miller is clear that, ultimately, the manner of decision making on this issue showcased the weakness of Bush's delegatory approach:

> If you are the president and you've been told something like we are not going to disband the Iraqi army because a lot of bad things will happen, when Bremer comes in and says we're going to disband the army, at the very least you got to look around the table and say 'has anybody been in on this decision?'[22]

Bush wrote in his memoirs that 'In retrospect, I should have insisted on more debate on Jerry's orders … It is possible we would have issued the orders anyway. They were tough calls, and any alternative would have created a separate set of problems … But the discussion would have better prepared us for what followed.'[23]

Bush's tendency to delegate and Rumsfeld's uneven management of Bremer allowed the CPA chief to exercise substantial discretion in making major policy decisions during the early post-war. The net result of disbanding the army, as with the decision not to implement the IIA concept, was to ensure a full-scale, lengthy US occupation. Another key pillar of US post-war policy had changed without serious engagement by either the president or the secretary of defence. Bremer was criticized for this decision, and it is true that he took the crucial steps. But Bush and Rumsfeld could have overruled him and insisted upon a different policy.

The path to sovereignty

Bush and Rumsfeld differed over how stable and democratic Iraq had to be before the US could depart. These differences were characteristically fudged as the CPA planned for the transfer of sovereignty to an Iraqi government. The president's position was generally supportive of what the CPA was doing but lacked detailed guidance. Bush's view was that the US should stay as long as the job took. This left a wide swath of interpretive possibility. Rumsfeld vacillated on the issue of sovereignty. Before Bremer's appointment, he had been in favour of a quick handover. He had retreated from this position at the crucial point that Bremer was hired and given instruction. By September 2003, he was in favour, again, of a rapid transition. By that point, though, Bremer had formalized an occupation.

Two op-ed pieces published a few days apart in the *Washington Post* showed the range of possibilities from the perspective of Baghdad. First came the view from the Iraqi Governing Council, set up by Bremer to work alongside the CPA. This piece was written by Ahmad Chalabi, the Iraqi leader most vocal in pushing for an early transfer of power.

> The Iraqi people must feel they have a stake in their governance; they must feel that they are in control of their own land. Iraqis welcome liberation but reject occupation. The key to empowering the Iraqi people to win back their homeland is the restoration of Iraqi sovereignty. The people need to see an accelerated timetable for the restoration of sovereignty to reinforce the national pride and self-respect that stem from self-government. The politics of occupation is well practiced in the Middle East – the coalition would be wise to avoid it.[24]

The second op-ed came, eight days later, from Bremer himself. It was greeted with widespread shock, and not only from Iraqis. The CPA, Bremer wrote in 'Iraq's path to sovereignty', would oversee a long-term, multi-stage process.[25] Bremer began with sentiments Chalabi would agree with: 'Occupation is unpopular with occupier and occupied alike. We believe Iraqis should be given responsibility for their own security, economic development and political system as soon as possible.'

However, Bremer continued, the transfer of sovereignty required elections and a constitution, and there were formidable barriers to both. In Iraq at that point there were 'no election rolls, no election law, no political parties' law and no electoral districts'. The existing constitution was 'a Hussein-dictated formula for tyranny'. The transfer of sovereignty would take several years, meaning CPA would constitute the government for the foreseeable future.

As with abandoning the IIA and disbanding the army, Bremer felt that he had some freedom of manoeuvre from Washington on this. Rumsfeld had been inconsistent on the issue, and was by now much more concerned with standing up new Iraqi security forces so that US troops could be withdrawn.[26] Visiting Bremer a few days before his op-ed appeared, the two barely discussed the issue of the transfer of sovereignty and governance. Instead, Bremer received a classic Rumsfeld motivational talk, focused on the speed of training of security forces. 'I don't see a steady line of advance,' Rumsfeld told a deeply irritated Bremer. 'Maybe we need better metrics... I wonder if all of you working here have a sufficient sense of urgency.'[27] Whereas Gen. Franks had redoubled his efforts after being spoken to in this way by Rumsfeld, Bremer concluded that the secretary was not being empathetic and decided to maintain a greater distance from him.

The president still had not given Bremer detailed guidance on the process of transferring power to an Iraqi government. He had said to Bremer repeatedly that his commitment to him, the CPA, and the whole enterprise was valid 'until the job is done'. As with the guidance on the Iraqi Interim Authority, Bremer interpreted these supportive comments as constituting presidential permission to use his best judgement.

Douglas Feith, by now very sensitive to Bremer's tendency to freelance, could not believe what he was reading in the newspaper. 'It was a major policy statement – and one that Bremer had not cleared with anyone in the Pentagon. The piece amazed me.'[28] The path to sovereignty was fundamental to the US enterprise in Iraq, whether measured against the president's goals of democratization or Rumsfeld's goal of withdrawal. The issues Bremer confronted of sequencing, and the trade-off between speed and legitimacy, were fundamental in nature and deserved the sustained attention of the National Security Council. Yet Bremer came up with the policy without clear and sustained guidance from either Bush or Rumsfeld.

Bremer's op-ed, though, did get their attention. Rumsfeld was told of it whilst on a military plane returning from visits to Iraq and Afghanistan. 'This was the first I'd heard of the article's existence. In fact, I had just spent two days in Baghdad with Bremer, and he had mentioned nothing about it, nor had he even hinted at the star-tling news [of a multi-year occupation] it contained.'[29] Feith wrote that the op-ed made Rumsfeld 're-think his relationship with Bremer. The article, in effect, mocked the idea that Bremer worked for him'. Stung into action, the secretary of defence undertook the 'first – and arguably the only – major intervention […] to overrule Bremer'.

Directly overruling was not Rumsfeld's style. With Franks, he had been able to chivvy, suggest, coax, question and goad. The general had responded well, striving to give Rumsfeld what he wanted. But Franks was a military man with a clear chain of command and the inclination to follow it. In the case of the war plan, there had been time to go through multiple iterations, and everything was done through written documentation and regular close interaction – Rumsfeld's preferred methods.

Bremer did not have the same clarity on the chain of command as Franks – he believed he was the president's agent, and this permitted him to ignore Rumsfeld. The secretary had given Bremer contradictory signals on the sovereignty issue, in contrast to the consistency with which he had pushed Franks in the preferred direction. Rumsfeld's approach annoyed Bremer, who believed himself to be the independent executive of a foreign country rather than a field commander subor-dinate to the secretary of defence. 'As the months went on,' Rumsfeld later recalled, 'it was clear that when I made suggestions to Bremer, he did not take them well. His formal direction to report through me was being ignored. He was receiving guid-ance directly from many in the administration – the president, Rice, Powell – and choosing which guidance he preferred. After four months of what looked to me to be a series of unfortunate decisions, I felt a need to intervene.'[30]

Rumsfeld re-engaged with post-war governance in Iraq, and swung back to his original position – a quick hand-off. He called Bremer on 13 September to press for granting sovereignty to either the Governing Council or 'some other group of Iraqis'. Bremer 'told him bluntly that I disagreed'. Rumsfeld's reply was characteristic of his work style: 'Well, then, send me a paper giving me your reasons.'[31] Bremer was called back to Washington. Bremer dismissed a paper he was given on quickly turning the Governing Council into a provisional government as 'old fish in a new wrapper'.[32] He had undone the Iraqi Interim Authority concept once, and would not revive it now.

Condoleezza Rice was also awakened by Bremer's op-ed. She called Bremer, and asked him to consider a much quicker timetable and handing over to the Governing Council – effectively coming into line with the Pentagon's proposal. 'I don't think the political situation in Washington will support another year' of occupation, she told him. 'Can we put together some kind of a provisional government?' With Colin Powell also alarmed at the length of Bremer's timetable, the ambassador was left to reflect that 'every single member of the president's foreign policy team had pushed this idea at me over the last three weeks'.[33]

To Paul Bremer, though, this did not mean that he was obliged to act upon it. Bremer was being handled more strongly by Rice now – she was even elbowing Rumsfeld out of the way in the process. Rice called back to service her old colleague from the George H.W. Bush years, Robert Blackwill, who as Ambassador to India had equal rank to Bremer and was equally assertive. She announced that she was creating an 'Iraq Stabilization Group' to run Bremer from within the NSC, and that Blackwill would journey to Iraq to be the group's enforcer, and to help Bremer achieve an earlier transfer of sovereignty.

Rumsfeld responded testily to this encroachment on his turf. He sent a strongly worded memo to the president's chief of staff, Andy Card, disputing Rice's suggestion that he had concurred with the creation of the Iraq Stabilization Group. It began, 'In Monday's [news]paper, Condi, in effect, announced that the president is concerned about the post-war Iraq stabilization efforts and that, as a result, he has asked Condi Rice and the National Security Council to assume responsibility for post-war Iraq. The story indicates Condi stated that the reorganization was developed by herself, the vice president, Powell and Rumsfeld. I was not consulted—only advised.'

Although he was annoyed by the manner of the announcement, Rumsfeld sensed an opportunity to have responsibility for Bremer shifted elsewhere. After all, he wrote, Bremer was increasingly doing non-Department of Defence types of things, such as politics and economics, he was reporting to others in the administration anyway, and given Rice's public announcement '[t]o not make the transfer now [in the super-vision of Bremer] will cause confusion.'[34] Asked by a journalist to explain why the changes where necessary, he responded that he didn't know: 'I think you have to ask Condi that question.' Unwisely, the reporter persisted in the questioning. 'I said

I don't know. *Isn't that clear? Don't you understand English?*[35] The episode reflected multiple aspects of Rumsfeld's personality and leadership style. He distrusted the NSC, and was a traditionalist in terms of the chain of command. This was more than just a lack of respect for Rice's skills and intellect, although clearly that factored in.

Bush and Rumsfeld handled the re-education of Bremer in their characteristic ways. Rumsfeld contributed an elliptically argued memo entitled 'Risk in the Way Ahead in Iraq'. He stated that 'there is a tension with respect to the pace at which sovereignty is moved to the Iraqis'. He then laid out the options for and against an accelerated transfer. The issue was complex, he thought. On the one hand, 'To the extent we move quickly and give sovereignty to the Iraqis, there is a risk that the preparations may prove to have been inadequate. As a result, there could be a diminution in the US ability to see that the eventual Iraqi government is within the president's redlines and fits the model he has described.' On the other hand, 'Moving too slowly with respect to passing sovereignty to the Iraqis risks having the center of gravity of the Iraqi population move against the Coalition, their coopera- tion decline, Iraqis become afraid of joining the police, the Governing Council, etc. and be more likely to work with our enemies.'[36]

The president had given Rice authority to create the ISG and appoint Blackwill, and agreed to the recommendation that Bremer should abandon his insistence on holding full elections and writing a constitution prior to turning over sovereignty.[37] However, in the full National Security Council session, Bush was more cheerlead- ing. In Bremer's account of the meeting, the president heard the options – Bremer's suggestion of a long, sequential process and the Pentagon's preference for a quick handover – and 'did not commit himself'. At the end of the meeting, he offered a statement of resolve:

> We are going to succeed in Iraq despite the difficult times we are going through. Nobody should be in any doubt. We will do the right thing irrespective of what the newspapers or political opponents say about it. Success in Iraq will change the world. The American people need to have no doubt that we're confident about the outcome. We may not succeed by the time of the [2004 US presidential] election. So be it.

For Bremer, 'That was all the guidance I needed'[38] – but it was no real guidance at all. The lessons of the IIA – that it was dangerous to offer support without specific instructions to Paul Bremer – had not been fully absorbed. Bush never confronted the ambassador directly. Indeed, not only did Bremer leave Washington with the pres- ident's private praise, he was also rewarded days later with a saccharine *Washington Post* story about how much Bush valued his counsel and how close the two were.[39]

Conceptualizing the insurgency

These august questions of sovereignty were debated against a backdrop of violence. An insurgency, at first led by disenfranchised Sunnis, began to grow in the summer of 2003. Rumsfeld responded to the violence in analytical fashion, focusing on whether it merited the label 'insurgency'. He tasked his aide, Steve Bucci, with locating the Department of Defence *Dictionary of Military and Associated Terms*. Rumsfeld asked Bucci to give him the terms for 'insurgency, guerrilla war, and belligerency. Each on a separate sheet of paper'.[40] The secretary continued to be concerned with labelling the issue several months later, writing to Wolfowitz, Abizaid, Bremer and Feith:

> [T]he terminology we use is enormously important. The fact that so many of our folks are talking about the situation in Iraq as a 'guerrilla war,' with the word 'guerrilla' having a positive connotation in some people's minds, is unfortunate. So too, the use of the phrase 'former regime loyalist' is unfortunate in that 'loyalist' has a positive connotation. The use of the phrase 'Sunni Triangle' in a negative sense is harmful to our efforts with the Sunnis. We have to do a better job of using words that are well thought through and calculated to express exactly what we mean. The word 'fanatic' has a negative connotation. The word 'terrorist' has a negative connotation in most cases. I hope you will continue thinking through what words we ought to use to describe the people who are causing us the difficulties in Iraq and come back with some suggestions that we can all then use.[41]

In his memoirs, he wrote that the proper label for the resistance was a 'Baathist-Jihadist axis' that 'was less of an insurgency – an armed political movement that arose organically from the general population – and more a counterrevolution'.[42]

Bush did not parse concepts. He responded emotionally. On 2 July, he told the press, 'There are some who feel that the conditions are such that they can attack us there. My answer is: Bring 'em on. We've got the force necessary to deal with the security situation.'[43]

Notes

1 Donald H. Rumsfeld, *Known and Unknown* (New York: Sentinel, 2011), 508.
2 Special Inspector General for Iraq Reconstruction, *Hard Lessons: The Iraq Reconstruction Experience*, 96. Available at www.sigir.mil/applyinghardlessons/index.html.
3 James Dobbins, *Occupying Iraq: A History of the Coalition Provisional Authority* (Santa Monica, CA: RAND Corporation, 2009): 13. Available at www.rand.org/pubs/monographs/2009/RAND_MG847.pdf.
4 Dobbins, *Occupying Iraq*, 14
5 Dobbins, *Occupying Iraq*, 18.
6 Dobbins, *Occupying Iraq*, 24–25.
7 Donald H. Rumsfeld, *Known and Unknown* (New York: Sentinel, 2011), 513.
8 Michael R. Gordon, 'Fateful Choices on Iraq Army Bypassed Debate', *New York Times*, 17 March 2008, www.nytimes.com/2008/03/17/world/middleeast/17bremer.html.
9 Michael R. Gordon, 'Debate Lingering on Decision to Dissolve the Iraqi Military', *New York Times*, 21 October 2004, http://query.nytimes.com/gst/fullpage.html?res=9E04E2DB113 AF932A15753C1A9629C8B63&pagewanted=all.

10   Department of Defense briefing, 'Rebuilding the Iraqi Military', 21 January 2003. Available
     at www.waranddecision.com/docLib/20080420_RebuildingIraqiMilitary.pdf.

11   Douglas J. Feith, *War and Decision: Inside the Pentagon at the Dawn of the War on Terror*
     (New York: Harper, 2008), 367–368.

12   Bremer's view is set out most completely in his op-ed 'How I Didn't Dismantle Iraq's
     Army', *New York Times*, 6 September 2007, available at www.nytimes.com/2007/09/06/
     opinion/06bremer.html.

13   Feith, *War and Decision*, 432.

14   Bremer, 'How I Didn't Dismantle Iraq's Army'; see also L. Paul Bremer to Rumsfeld et al.,
     'Dissolution of the Ministry of Defense and Related Entities', 19 May 2003. Available at
     http://library.Rumsfeld.com/doclib/sp/340/2003-05-19%20from%20Bremer%20re%20
     Dissolution%20of%20the%20Ministry%20of%20Defense%20and%20related%20Entities.
     pdf.

15   L. Paul Bremer to President George W. Bush, 22 May 2003. Available at www.nytimes.com/
     ref/washington/04bremer-text1.html.

16   Edmund L. Andrews, 'Envoy's Letter Counters Bush on Dismantling of Iraq Army',
     New York Times, 4 September 2007. Available at www.nytimes.com/2007/09/04/
     washington/04bremer.html?pagewanted=print.

17   Robert Draper, *Dead Certain: The Presidency of George W. Bush* (New York: Free Press,
     2007), 207.

18   Peter Rodman to Donald Rumsfeld, 'Disbanding the Iraqi Army', 24 May 2006. Available
     at   http://library.Rumsfeld.com/doclib/sp/339/2006-05-24%20from%20Rodman%20
     re%20Disbanding%20the%20Iraqi%20Army.pdf.

19   US Department of Defence, 'Secretary of Defense Donald Rumsfeld Interviews with
     Mr. Bob Woodward, July 6 and 7 2006', www.defense.gov/transcripts/transcript.aspx?
     transcriptid=3744.

20   Rumsfeld, *Known and Unknown*, 518.

21   Author interview with Miller.

22   Author interview with Miller.

23   George W. Bush, *Decision Points* (New York: Random House, 2011), 259–260.

24   Ahmad Chalabi, 'The View From Iraq', *The Washington Post*, 31 August 2003, B7.

25   L. Paul Bremer III, 'Iraq's Path to Sovereignty', *The Washington Post*, 8 September 2003, A21.

26   Dana Priest, 'Iraqi Role Grows In Security Forces; Rumsfeld Says Ranks to Swell Rapidly',
     The Washington Post, 5 September 2003, 16.

27   Bremer, *My Year in Iraq*, 156.

28   Feith, *War and Decision*, 453.

29   Rumsfeld, *Known and Unknown*, 522.

30   Rumsfeld, *Known and Unknown*, 522.

31   Bremer, *My Year in Iraq*, 167.

32   Bremer, *My Year in Iraq*, 170.

33   Bremer, *My Year in Iraq*, 188.

34   Rumsfeld to Bush et al., 'Iraq Reporting Relationships', 6 October 2003. http://library.
     Rumsfeld.com/doclib/sp/355/2003-10-06%20to%20President%20George%20W%20
     Bush%20re%20Iraq%20Reporting%20Relationships.pdf.

35   Mike Allen, 'Iraq shake-up skipped Rumsfeld; Confidential Memo was first alert, Defense
     Secretary Says', *The Washington Post*, 8 October 2003, 10.

36   Rumsfeld, 'Risk in the way ahead in Iraq', 28 October 2003. http://library.Rumsfeld.com/
     doclib/sp/353/re%20Risk%20in%20the%20Way%20Ahead%20in%20Iraq%2010-28-
     2003.pdf.

37   Feith, *War and Decision*, 464–465.

38   Bremer, *My Year in Iraq*, 207.

39   Robin Wright and Glenn Kessler, 'Rapport Between Bush, Bremer Grows; President Relies on Counsel of Top US Envoy to Iraq, Officials Say', *The Washington Post*, 23 November 2003, 23.

40   Rumsfeld to Steven Bucci, 'DoD Dictionary', 23 July 2003. http://library.Rumsfeld. com/doclib/sp/347/2003-07-23%20to%20Steve%20Bucci%20re%20DoD%20 Dictionary-%20Memo%20Attachment.pdf.

41   Rumsfeld to Wolfowitz et al., 'Terminology', 7 January 2004. http://library.Rumsfeld.com/ doclib/sp/349/To%20Paul%20Wolfowitz%20re%20Terminology%2001-07-2004.pdf.

42   Rumsfeld, *Known and Unknown*, 675.

43   Thomas E. Ricks, *Fiasco: The American Military Adventure in Iraq* (New York: Penguin, 2006), 172.

7

Rumsfeld's exit strategy

From the end of the Coalition Provisional Authority to the decision to surge, Bush and Rumsfeld allowed US policy in Iraq to drift. They were unable to improve the security situation and establish a viable Iraqi government. The contradictions between the president's approach and the secretary of defence's approach contributed to these problems.

This chapter covers Iraq policy from June 2004 until mid-2006 from the standpoint of security and of politics, analyzing Bush and Rumsfeld's conceptions of what was necessary and the conflict between these two visions. Bush and Rumsfeld's worldviews led them to very different conclusions as to what was required, but their personal styles meant that they did not have a direct debate about these differences. The puzzling US behaviour during this period – describing Iraq as central to the war on terror and the spread of democracy, yet simultaneously drawing down forces and planning to leave – is revealed here as a product of the conflict between the visions of Bush and Rumsfeld.

President Bush placed responsibility for Iraq on US shoulders. In the security realm, he saw combating the insurgency as a US task that was within the capacity of the military to achieve. But he did not give clear guidance on how to accomplish this, nor did he ensure that Rumsfeld and the commanding General George Casey were executing a plan that would achieve his goals. In the political realm, Bush wanted Iraq to be the centrepiece of his Freedom Agenda, an example of democracy that would radiate out across the Middle East. He insisted that free elections go ahead on schedule.

Rumsfeld, by contrast, felt that the continued insurgency in Iraq should not lead to long-term US involvement. His goal was to achieve a quick and orderly withdrawal of forces. Security in Iraq was a complex problem that was mostly beyond the influence of the US, certainly at an acceptable cost. He coaxed and prodded General Casey toward this viewpoint and encouraged him to withdraw troops as quickly as possible. In the political realm, Rumsfeld felt that once an Iraqi government had been appointed, that should be the end of US involvement. The Iraqis should shape their own political situation. If that turned out to involve an autocratic model rather than a democracy, it was not the concern of the US. Whilst seeking military withdrawal from Iraq, Rumsfeld also worked during this period to minimize the responsibility of the Pentagon for making Iraq policy.

Table 7.1 details the effect of Bush and Rumsfeld's individual characteristics on Iraq policy during this period.

Politics: forging an Iraqi government

On 28 May 2004, Ayad Allawi, a former Iraqi dissident whom Saddam had once tried to have killed, was announced as prime minister. Allawi would head an interim government whilst Iraq prepared for the elections of January 2005. President Bush played virtually no role in the selection of Allawi. Asked about his involvement, Bush told reporters: 'I had no role. I mean, occasionally, somebody said this person

Table 7.1 Rumsfeld's exit strategy

Bush's traits	Exit strategy	Rumsfeld's traits	Exit strategy
Black-and-white worldview	Iraq reframed as emblematic war for democracy, of generational and global importance. Insistence on no postponement of elections.	Complex worldview	Problem in Iraq complex, about more than just security. Defines Clear, Hold, Build in complex terms, altering meaning of strategy.
History maker	Believes creating acceptable security situation is US responsibility. Supports Clear, Hold, Build.	History manager	Believes Iraqi government should stand or fall on its own. Favours 'strongman' Iraqi government model. Opposes Clear, Hold, Build.
Cheerleading interpersonal style	Supports Casey.	Prosecutorial interpersonal style	Fights with Rice over policy turf.
Delegator	Asks few questions of Casey and Rumsfeld's drawdown plan. Does not enforce will on Clear, Hold, Build.	Dictator or delegator	Coaxes Casey toward drawdown plan without giving firm guidance. Tries to reduce Pentagon responsibility for Iraq.

may be interested, or that – but I had no role in picking, zero.'[1] The president saw this appointed interim government as a necessary intermediary step toward the full democracy he envisioned for Iraq.

Rumsfeld thought that the advent of the Allawi government should mark the end of US obligations in Iraq. Saddam had gone, the CPA was over, and US forces should play a circumscribed and diminishing role in the country. 'With the end of the CPA,' he wrote, 'we had returned to our original emphasis on more modest goals – keeping the nation reasonably secure and enabling the Iraqis to defeat the insurgency over time.'[2] Rumsfeld circulated a memo to senior Pentagon officials indicating that they should pass off many elements of Iraq policy onto other government agencies. 'We regularly have PCs and NSCs on Iraq, where the Pentagon always briefs,' he wrote. 'There is a great deal more going on in Iraq beyond security... We ought to suggest to the NSC... that other departments should put together briefings on other subjects of interest. We need to make it clear that Iraq is not simply a security issue.'[3]

Elections

The interim Allawi government was charged with arranging its own demise in favour of an elected successor. Elections were to take place no later than the end of January 2005. As the elections approached, there was almost constant speculation that they would be postponed. Political leaders of the Sunni minority insisted they would encourage a boycott of elections which were sure to enshrine their new out-of-power status. The Sunni insurgency wanted to render the security situation untenable so that elections could not be held.

The Iraqi Interim Government itself was ambivalent about allowing the vote to occur. The best outcome possible for them was that they would be returned to jobs they already held. As Ali Allawi recalls, 'In private, the leading luminaries in the Interim Government expressed their deep misgivings about democracy and whether it could ever take root in the rocky terrain of Iraq.'[4] Prime Minister Ayad Allawi was not at core a democrat, according to his cousin Ali. Ayad Allawi's preferred model for Iraq was:

> [t]he ruling political elite would comprise 'reformed Baathists', a professional and high-status officer class, and a group of apolitical technocrats in charge of the economy and the service ministries. Security would be provided through a revitalized intelligence apparatus, perhaps not as heavy-handed as before, but equally intrusive and pervasive. Tribes, or at least tribal leaders, would be co-opted into the process by the liberal use of large cash handouts... liberties would be curtailed, but domestic stability would be ensured.[5]

This would have been an acceptable outcome for Rumsfeld, whose prime concern was extricating the armed forces from Iraq. Peter Wehner, the White House director of strategic initiatives, said that Rumsfeld would have been comfortable with the 'strongman' model as an exit strategy.[6]

By contrast, most Shia subscribed to the logic that elections are good if your group constitutes the majority.[7] Ibrahim Jaafari of the Shiite Dawa party put it succinctly: 'My fear is there will be no election, not the results of the election.'[8] While Sunni leaders were telling their followers to boycott, the Shia leader Ayatollah Sistani labelled non-voting 'a form of high treason'. Participation in the elections, a Sistani ally said in a compelling get-out-the-vote message, 'has religious sanctity and abstention will throw the transgressor into hellfire'.[9]

Given likely Sunni abstention, Interim Government ambivalence, and the security considerations, there were compelling arguments in favour of postponing the elections. Bush's commitment to democracy in Iraq, and his sheer stubbornness, were crucial factors in ensuring that there was no postponement. On 4 January 2005, Ayad Allawi called Bush to discuss the impediments to holding elections on time – a conversation that was designed to lay the groundwork for a postponement. 'Clearly the thinking on this is still in motion in Baghdad,' said a senior administration official, but 'President Bush is holding firm.'[10] Allawi reported that an 'overwhelming majority' of the Interim Government favoured postponement of elections, and, in public, the Vice President Ghazi al-Yawar said the choice was a 'tough call'.[11]

Bush reiterated his belief that the path to success in Iraq was to push ahead with democracy. 'Democracy is hard ... but it's hard for a reason. And the reason it's hard is because there are a handful of folks who fear freedom.'[12] Bush's recent re-election had left him with little incentive to compromise on his central policy. Asked by the *Washington Post* whether the war in Iraq had gone badly, he refused to engage with the question: 'We had an accountability moment, and that's called the 2004 elections. The American people listened to different assessments made about what was taking place in Iraq, and they looked at the two candidates, and they chose me.'[13]

The president's personal commitment to the elections going forward as scheduled was crucial in avoiding a postponement. As Ali Allawi notes of the election sceptics in the Interim Government, 'in public they were bound to pay more than lip service to the notion of electoral democracy, if for no other reason than that was what the president of the United States had publicly demanded.'[14] Whilst Rumsfeld would have been happy to endorse Ayad Allawi as a strongman if it allowed for a quick exit, Bush was not prepared to compromise on the issue of holding the elections on time.

Security: US strategy and training Iraqi forces

Bush and Rumsfeld also differed on security policy. In June 2004 General Ricardo Sanchez was replaced by General George Casey as commander of allied forces in Iraq. Casey and Rumsfeld met to speak about the campaign objectives prior to the general's deployment. The secretary was clear that, in his mind, the mission was not to remake Iraq. Casey should concentrate on withdrawing US forces as soon as possible. Don't try and fix the country, Rumsfeld warned him, make the Iraqis do it for themselves.[15] At the same time, President Bush was explaining to the American people that Iraq was the key conflict of the generation, and the centrepiece of an ambitious democratization agenda. Bush, though, spent little time with Casey, again missing an opportunity to ensure that the approach of his military in Iraq matched the goals that he was setting.

General Casey agreed with Rumsfeld that the US military should not try to solve all of Iraq's problems.[16] For the first period of his campaign, from July 2004 to the national elections at the end of January 2005, Casey developed two objectives. First, insurgent safe havens, such as Najaf and Fallujah, had to be cleared. Ideally, this would be done with the interim Iraqi government taking the political lead, and Iraqi security forces playing a major role in the actual fighting. Second, training of the Iraqi army and police had to be accelerated, so that the government elected in January 2005 would have the tools necessary to secure the country.[17] Then the Iraqi government would gain legitimacy and capacity, violence would decline, and US troops could be withdrawn.

When Casey presented his written campaign plan to Rumsfeld, the secretary agreed with the basic approach, but characteristically argued with Casey about specifics of language. The word 'faltering', as in progress, should be replaced by 'slow', whilst the goals of 'isolating the insurgency'; 'ensuring popular support' and 'applying military power' were prefaced at Rumsfeld's insistence with 'help Iraqis in….'.[18] The counter-insurgency fight, Rumsfeld hoped, would now be subject to some 'Iraqi-ization'.[19] As was so often the case with Rumsfeld, his interest in the precise use of language was a means by which he sought to impart serious guidance on strategic matters.

The second phase of the campaign under Casey began after the January 2005 elections. US troop levels had surged briefly to provide extra security for the election, but an elected government was now in place, and a permanent constitution ratified. Rumsfeld wanted to accelerate the process of withdrawal. He believed that a political solution would lead to a security solution, and so it was time to pull back US forces. The secretary could not see a compelling reason for continued US involvement, and believed that the US presence was fuelling the insurgency.

Rumsfeld's motivations were three-fold. First, he wanted to extricate the military from Iraq in order to focus on moving toward a lighter, more flexible force. Rumsfeld was under pressure from some in the Army leadership to permanently expand the size of the force if it was going to be deployed at current levels, and as he was against such an expansion, he had to reduce the level of deployment.[20]

Second, Rumsfeld hated expenditure of any kind, and was particularly chagrined by tasks that called for a lot of manpower. He believed that the army always over-estimated the number of personnel it needed to achieve any task, and strong leadership from the top was necessary in order to prune requests to a more reasonable level. 'If we leave Department of Defense to its own devices,' he had written in a memo to senior Pentagon leadership, 'we will end up dipping into the taxpayers' money and using DoD military personnel because it is easier, they are there and it seems to be a bottomless pit – but it isn't, it can't be, and it shouldn't be.'[21]

Third, he believed that a heavy US troop presence would retard the development of Iraqis in terms of both security forces and political maturity. He would constantly refer to the 'hand on the bicycle seat' problem: a child masters riding a bike only after the parent removes the stabilizing hand. Even if the child crashes once or twice, that is the only way independence can be achieved.

Rumsfeld's fundamental belief concerning the Iraqi insurgency, then, was that the Iraqis themselves had to solve it. Rumsfeld, a history manager, felt the US could not defeat it for them. As he wrote to his speechwriter Matt Latimer:

> Let's prepare a statement that says: If the Iraqi people don't stop other Iraqis from destroying infrastructure, preventing the investment in infrastructure, preventing construction and projects to help the Iraqi people; and if the Iraqi people don't provide the intelligence to the Iraqi Security Forces so they can stop terrorists from destroying their country, then they are going to live in a destroyed country. It's not complicated. It's their country; they are going to have to do it; nobody is going to do it for them. The US cannot do it for them; neither can the Coalition, the UN, or anybody else. They better get about it.[22]

Rumsfeld would press his generals to concur that US forces should be drawn-down, whilst at the same time seeking to have others take up the burden of fighting the insurgents by accelerating the training of Iraqi forces and seeking additional troops from US allies.

Casey briefed Rumsfeld on 27 January 2005 on his post-election security plan, using a chart indicating the pace of the drawdown of troops. Rumsfeld responded that the 'line does not feel right to me…the slope (of drawdown) is not steep enough'. This prodding, reminiscent of Rumsfeld's interactions with Gen. Tommy Franks, produced the desired effect, and when the secretary visited in person two weeks later, Casey was talking of a reduction to as few as six US combat brigades in Iraq by the end of 2005. 'He was always pushing us to go faster with the transitions,' Casey told Rumsfeld's biographer Bradley Graham: 'There's no question that he [Rumsfeld] thought faster reductions were better.'[23]

Rumsfeld did not have to bully his generals in order to have them accept this approach.[24] The CENTCOM commander General John Abizaid and General Casey both agreed with the policy, although for different reasons. Abizaid, who as CENTCOM commander saw Iraq within a wider strategic context, believed that the current US force levels were unsustainable over the long term. He believed, though, that the US could not just withdraw, but should instead concentrate its efforts on training Iraqi forces. This program should be significantly stepped up, with many more US trainers embedded with Iraqi units.[25]

General Casey had been vice chief of staff of the army before being deployed to Iraq and he took the perspective of his old job with him to his new one. A key goal for him was to not wreck the army in Iraq. He agreed with Rumsfeld that US troops served as a hand on the bicycle seat. Casey also thought Iraq would swallow as many troops as the US sent – there were an unlimited number of things for troops to do, but none of them would make the difference between victory and defeat. Iraq was a troop sump. Higher levels of US forces would serve as additional targets for insurgents, would discourage Iraqis from assuming responsibility, and would damage the morale and readiness of the US army.[26]

The violence had not abated during Casey's first months in Iraq. In consultation with Rumsfeld, he concluded that the insurgency was unwinnable by US forces. It was not spreading, but it was not being defeated either. In Casey's judgement, there was little prospect that a decisive victory could be achieved during the limited time the US population would support operations and the army could sustain them. The best that could be done was to pull out in a way that gave the Iraqis a fighting chance and minimized the damage done to the army. While he had previously outlined a best-case scenario of drawdown to six brigades by the end of 2005, this was now unachievable. The new timeline was to drawdown to fifteen brigades by January 2006, thirteen brigades six months later, and ten brigades by the end of 2006. Troops were to be consolidated on giant 'Forward Operating Bases' on the outskirts of cities, with the number of US troop bases dropping from ninety-two to just four.[27] Rumsfeld fully agreed with this. Rumsfeld biographer Bradley Graham examined communications between Rumsfeld and Casey:

> There is nothing in the files of the message traffic between the secretary and Casey indicating that, with each other, they fundamentally questioned the strategy being pursued. To the contrary, they figured that if they could just get to the election of a new Iraqi government at the end of 2005 and see steady improvement in Iraq's security forces, they could turn the corner in the war.[28]

President Bush, though, had a different view, and this goes to the core of the difference between him and Rumsfeld at this point. When Casey briefed Bush in March 2005 that the best course of action was to concentrate on training Iraqi troops, given that the average counter-insurgency effort took around a decade to succeed and the US could not stay in Iraq that long, Bush registered his concern. 'George, we're not playing for a tie. I want to make sure we understand this, don't we?'[29] Casey responded that he did understand, and Bush did not follow up. This was a crucial moment for Bush. He had begun to ascertain that there was a disjunction between his strategic goals and the briefings he was receiving from his field commander. But the president too easily accepted the assurances of a subordinate that all was well, and failed to look into the matter further for many months.

Clear, Hold, Build: stirrings against the Rumsfeld/Casey plan

Casey had concluded the insurgency could not be defeated within a reasonable time frame, and Rumsfeld wanted to leave. A plan for a gradual drawdown, whilst Iraqi forces were standing up, was in place. In the meantime, Casey and Rumsfeld hoped to minimize US casualties, and maximize the development of Iraqi forces, by concentrating troops on large Forward Operating Bases (FOBs) on the edges of urban areas. They would be available for major operations, but not day-to-day policing of the sectarian troubles.

The president was committed to winning and to promoting democracy in Iraq. The secretary of defence was not so committed, and in consultation with the commanding General had developed a policy of force protection and drawdown. There was still a mismatch between the means provided by Rumsfeld and Casey and the ends desired by Bush.

In the absence of a genuine debate and resolution to the conflict in Washington, DC, ad hoc attempts to bridge the gap between means and ends emerged in the field. In the spring of 2005, Colonel H.R. McMaster's 3rd Armoured Cavalry division swept into the northwestern Iraqi town of Tal Afar and, instead of retreating to their Forward Operating Base, maintained a presence in order to ensure insurgents did not return – a shift toward classic counter-insurgency tactics that would, if replicated nationwide, require significantly greater numbers of US troops in Iraq.[30] In the State Department, Counsellor to the Secretary Phillip Zelikow took note of the Tal Afar success.[31] Zelikow wrote a memo to Rice suggesting that the Tal Afar strategy be applied generally in Iraq, and prepared the secretary's congressional testimony in October 2005 where she announced it as the administration's posture. Zelikow recalls that

> Her testimony to the Congress in October '05 is very consciously written as an effort to articulate a strategy for success in Iraq, because we had felt for sometime that we weren't doing that effectively for the American people. In some ways we were beginning to be more and more worried that we weren't doing it enough internally. Ideally the White House would articulate this. And the president had been making a series of speeches, but for various reasons that they can best explain, the speeches just tended to be making the same kind of points the president had made before. I think even the president was restless with this. We looked around and said, 'We need to do this then, and the secretary will do it in her testimony.' That actually then spurred the White House to articulate the strategy.[32]

This approach became known as 'Clear, Hold, Build'. Under this new doctrine, US troops would remain in an area after clearing it of insurgents, holding the territory for long enough to help Iraqis build sustainable security, political and economic institutions. President Bush liked the plan and endorsed it, giving a series of speeches in support and having the White House Staff issue a high-profile document on the 'National Strategy for Victory in Iraq'.[33] However, whilst Bush endorsed the strategy rhetorically, he failed to take steps to ensure that it was implemented. This would have included a commitment of additional troops, and the president was not yet at the point where he recognized that this was necessary.

Rumsfeld thought that Clear, Hold, Build was an awful idea. The aim was to exit, not to hold and build:

> Anyone who takes those three words and thinks it means the United States should clear and the United States should hold and the United States should build doesn't understand the situation. It is the Iraqis' country. They've got 28 million people there. They are clearing, they are holding, they are building.[34]

He later told Bob Woodward 'they (the White House and State Department) felt that a bumper sticker was needed. I didn't need one'. Rumsfeld, characteristically, took issue with what he saw as linguistic imprecision: 'I was concerned that it had a connotation that sounded good at the moment, but that it could, over time, come back and – because of the nuances in it – not be seen right. So then we tried to define it. We left the words and we tried to define it in a way that was accurate.' Rumsfeld's preferred definition, however, changed the strategy fundamentally: 'it's not just us clearing, it's the coalition. And the holding – it's clearly increasingly them and not us. And the building is we want to help create environments so that they can reconstruct their own country, and that type of thing. And those refinements are in there now.'[35]

While Clear, Hold, Build was a cogent strategy, implementation was largely absent. As Zelikow recalls in frustration, 'we still were not building the underlying operational strategy that would give full body to the rhetoric'.[36] This was not by accident. Clear, Hold, Build was troop-intensive and required an obtrusive US military footprint – two things Rumsfeld and Casey sought to avoid. The Rumsfeld/Casey plan was based around the principle that the Iraqis would be the ones to achieve security goals and the objective was to showcase the effectiveness of the Iraqi government.[37]

Consequently, Clear, Hold, Build became, in effect, clear, let go, and leave, with Iraqi forces unable or unwilling to consolidate anti-insurgent gains made by the Americans. The president had endorsed Clear, Hold, Build and then failed to impose his will. As Frederick Kagan put it, 'the president has announced this strategy that the military then doesn't execute... that's a dysfunctional administration. Something's not working there if you've got the secretary of state enunciating a policy like that, the president adhering to it and endorsing it, and then the military commanders not executing. Something is broken.'[38] The key problem was that Rumsfeld did not support Clear, Hold, Build, and the president did not enforce his will.

US policy remained confused, a confusion caused by the different approaches toward the key questions of post-Saddam politics and security held by the president and the secretary of defence. Rumsfeld, in concert with General George Casey, had crafted a plan for withdrawal on the assumption that the US neither could, nor should, take the lead in defeating the insurgency. The president, meanwhile, continued to push his goals of democratization and military victory without perceiving the gap between means and ends that had arisen in Iraq. Only intermittently – when asking Casey to acknowledge that the US was pushing for 'a win, not a tie' and when endorsing the Clear, Hold, Build plan – did Bush accurately appraise the situation. In the following chapter, I analyze events that forced Bush to finally confront the basic differences between himself and his secretary of defence: the bombing of the mosque at Samarra, and the horrific spike in violence that followed.

Notes

1 'Remarks by the President on Iraqi Interim Government', 1 June 2004, available at http://georgewbush-whitehouse.archives.gov/news/releases/2004/06/print/ 20040601-2.html.

2 Donald H. Rumsfeld, *Known and Unknown* (New York, Sentinel, 2011), 672.

3 Bradley Graham, *By His Own Rules: The Ambitions, Successes, and Ultimate Failures of Donald Rumsfeld* (New York: Public Affairs, 2009), 489.

4 Ali A. Allawi, *The Occupation of Iraq: Winning the War, Losing the Peace* (New Haven, CT: Yale University Press, 2007), 330.

5 Allawi, *The Occupation of Iraq*, 337.

6 Author interview with Wehner.

7 Doug Struck and Bassam Sebti, 'Iraqi Shiite coalition tries to dispel fears of Iran-style rule', *Washington Post*, 16 January 2005, 21.

8 Karl Vick, 'Lottery sets order of ballot in Iraq; Officials alarmed by surge in violence', *Washington Post*, 21 December 2004, 18.

9 Allawi, *The Occupation of Iraq*, 343.

10 Richard A. Oppel Jr. and David E. Sanger, 'Iraqi Premier Calls Bush to Discuss Obstacles to Election', *New York Times*, 4 January 2005.

11 Dexter Filkins and David E. Sanger, 'Amid Tensions Iraqi Leader Affirms Jan 30 Vote Plan', *New York Times*, 6 January 2005.

12 David Stout, 'Bush Dismisses Growing Concerns Over Elections in Iraq', *New York Times*, 7 January 2005.

13 Jim VandeHei and Michael A. Fletcher, 'Bush says Election Ratified Iraq Policy', *Washington Post*, 16 January 2005, A1.

14 Allawi, *The Occupation of Iraq*, 330.

15 David Cloud and Greg Jaffe, *The Fourth Star: Four Generals and the Epic Struggle for the Future of the United States Army* (New York: Crown, 2009), 169.

16 Cloud and Jaffe, *The Fourth Star*, 170

17 Eric Schmitt, 'New US Commander Sees Shift in Military Role in Iraq', *New York Times*, 16 January 2005.

18 Graham, *By His Own Rules*, 491.

19 Robin Wright and Josh White, 'US Plans New Tack After Iraq Elections; Aim is to Accelerate Deployment of Iraqi Forces on Front Lines Against the Insurgents', *Washington Post*, 23 January 2005.

20   Eric Schmitt and Thom Shanker, 'Rumsfeld and Army Want to Delay Decision on Larger Force', *New York Times*, 5 February 2005, 19.

21   Rumsfeld to Feith et al., 'Foreign Troops', 20 February 2004. http://library.Rumsfeld.com/doclib/sp/427/To%20Doug%20Feith%20re%20Foreign%20Troops%2002-20-2004.pdf.

22   Rumsfeld to Matt Latimer, 'Statement on Iraq', 21 October 2004. http://library.Rumsfeld.com/doclib/sp/430/To%20Matt%20Latimer%20re%20Statement%20on%20Iraq%2010-21-2004.pdf.

23   Graham, *By His Own Rules*, 533.

24   Eric Schmitt, 'US Commanders See Possible Cut in Troops in Iraq', *New York Times*, 11 April 2005, 1.

25   Rumsfeld to Bush et al., 'Abizaid's Comments on Vickers' Paper', 22 June 2006. http://library.Rumsfeld.com/doclib/sp/465/2006-06-22%20to%20Bush%20re%20Abizaids%20comments%20on%20the%20paper%20by%20Mike%20Vickers.pdf; Graham, *By His Own Rules*, 535.

26   Cloud and Jaffe, *The Fourth Star*, 197.

27   Graham, *By His Own Rules*, 547.

28   Graham, *By His Own Rules*, 573.

29   Cloud and Jaffe, *The Fourth Star*, 192.

30   George Packer, 'Letter from Iraq: The Lesson of Tal Afar', *The New Yorker*, 10 April 2006, accessed at www.newyorker.com/archive/2006/04/10/060410fa_fact2.

31   *PBS Frontline* Interview with Phillip Zelikow. Available at www.pbs.org/wgbh/pages/frontline/endgame/interviews/zelikow.html#2, accessed 4 March 2008.

32   *PBS Frontline*, Interview with Zelikow.

33   National Security Council, *National Security Strategy for Victory in Iraq* (Washington, DC: White House, 2005). www.washingtonpost.com/wp-srv/nation/documents/Iraqnationalstrategy11-30-05.pdf.

34   'News Briefing with Secretary of Defense Donald Rumsfeld and Gen. Peter Pace', 29 November 2005, www.defenselink.mil/transcripts/transcript.aspx?transcriptid=1492.

35   US Department of Defence, 'Secretary of Defense Donald Rumsfeld interviews with Mr. Bob Woodward, July 6 and 7 2006'. Transcript available at www.defense.gov/Transcripts/Transcript.aspx?TranscriptID=3744.

36   *PBS Frontline*, Interview with Zelikow.

37   Graham, *By His Own Rules*, 490–491.

38   *PBS Frontline*, Interview with Frederick Kagan, www.pbs.org/wgbh/pages/frontline/endgame/interviews/kagan.html.

8

Bush takes charge

By sending additional troops to Iraq, a decision reached in late 2006 and announced 10 January 2007 – George W. Bush brought US strategy in line with his goals. Bush finally perceived that Rumsfeld's exit strategy was not going to achieve his aims of securing Iraq and paving the way for a democracy.[1]

In making the decision to surge, Bush defied the advice of Rumsfeld, the will of Congress, and the tide of public opinion. His decision was rooted in his personal characteristics. Bush conceptualized the situation in Iraq in stark winning/losing terms, and was unwilling to accept a compromise solution. His history maker temperament disposed him to believe that the troop surge could work, in stark contrast to much of the advice he received. His cheerleading interpersonal style led him to a positive relationship with the new Iraqi Prime Minister Nuri al-Maliki, whom he backed almost without reservation, again in contrast to advice he received from others concerning Maliki's effectiveness and trustworthiness.

By taking command here, elements of Bush's worldview overwhelmed his preferred management style of delegation. But this delegatory propensity was highly relevant to the timing of the surge. By delegating so much of the war to Rumsfeld and the generals, Bush had allowed a mismatch between his goals and US strategy to persist for a great deal of time. Now, he was correcting that.

Rumsfeld was opposed to the surge. He did not see Iraq in terms of the US winning or losing, nor did he see security as the core of the Iraq problem. For Rumsfeld, the Iraqi security situation was inextricably tied to the political, social and economic situation, and none of this was the responsibility of the US. No occupying power, in Rumsfeld's view, should or could solve these problems on behalf of another sovereign country. For Rumsfeld, the goal remained to leave in as orderly, as quick and as costless a way as possible. The Iraqis had failed to take control of their own situation. That may be tragic, Rumsfeld believed, but it was an Iraqi tragedy.

This period saw the parting of the ways between Bush and Rumsfeld. Table 8.1 offers an overview of how Bush and Rumsfeld's traits influenced surge decision making. The rest of the chapter details the accelerating deterioration of the situation in Iraq, as the failings of Rumsfeld's exit strategy became apparent. I then examine the process by which options for change were reviewed within the Bush administration, and the decisive intervention of the president on the side of the surge. I show

Table 8.1   The surge

Bush's traits	The surge	Rumsfeld's traits	The surge
Black-and-white worldview	Stark representation of alternatives. The 'Winning' heuristic – just bring me something that will work.	Complex worldview	Believes security problem more complex than just troop levels. Discursive contribution to definition of problem and delineation of options.
History maker	Believes surge can work. Refusal to leave Iraq to solve own problems.	History manager	Believes surge will not work. Believes US should leave Iraqis to solve own problems.
Cheerleading interpersonal style	Support for Maliki.	Prosecutorial interpersonal style	
Delegator	Long delay before strategy shift. Too-ready acceptance of reassurances of Rumsfeld, Casey.	Dictator or delegator?	Muddled approach to surge deliberations.

how the surge decision was driven by Bush's temperament, and how Rumsfeld's opposition to it was driven by his.

The aftermath of the Askariya shrine bombing

The events that would push the US to the brink of defeat in Iraq, and lead to the parting of the ways between Bush and Rumsfeld, began on 22 February 2006. The Askariya shrine, the most holy in Shiite Islam, was bombed by the Iraqi affiliate of Al-Qaeda, and its signature golden dome reduced to rubble. The Sunni group Al-Qaeda in Iraq had been trying to provoke a Sunni-Shiite civil war, and now seemed to have succeeded. There was an eruption of sectarian violence with hundreds killed, easily the worst since the invasion. Similar to the impact of the Tet offensive in Vietnam, the single event seemed to unravel much of the delicate political and security progress made over the previous two years.[2] While there was a brief period when it looked as though Shiite and Sunni had stared over the edge of the cliff and decided to draw back, the restraint did not last, and Iraq reached new heights of chaos, violence and killing.[3] This cut right to the heart of the Rumsfeld/ Casey plan. As Peter Feaver, a National Security Council official, explained:

> The core assumption [of the Rumsfeld / Casey plan] was that we would be able to get enough political progress, fast enough, to siphon off the Sunni insurgency and the Sunni anger about the government, the Sunni rejectionism, siphon that off fast enough that the problem that we are handing over to the Iraqis will be manageable. And so the pace that Defense was imagining [for withdrawal] was tolerable because we could create all this political progress, and the problem that we would be handing over to the Iraqis would be smaller than what we were facing at that point. So therefore even though they were less capable, they could manage it. That was the assumption, and that assumption was not borne out by events in 2006 with the Samarra bombing and the stalling of progress. You had the sectarian violence spiking, you had political progress stopping…and the strategy collapsed.[4]

Rumsfeld did not see the strategy as failing and in his view any remaining problems were for Iraqis, rather than the US, to solve. If the Iraqis could not make political progress that would lessen the insurgency, and their government's security forces were overwhelmed, then the US was absolved of responsibility and could not change the course of events in any case.[5] In Senate testimony on 9 March, Rumsfeld was clear that he did not want the US military in the middle of an Iraqi civil war: 'The plan is to prevent a civil war, and to the extent one were to occur, to have the – from a security standpoint – have the Iraqi security forces deal with it to the extent they're able to.'[6]

Bush's emphasis was different. He gave speeches in which he rejected the premise that the Iraqis should solve the problem alone and refused to retreat in the face of terrorists: 'They're hoping to shake our resolve and force us to retreat. They are not going to succeed.' Bush reaffirmed, at this moment of greatest challenge, his commitment to the grand democratizing vision that had underpinned, for him, the whole enterprise.

> By helping Iraqis build a democracy, we will deny the terrorists a safe haven to plan attacks against America. By helping Iraqis build a democracy, we will gain an ally in the war on terror. By helping Iraqis build a democracy, we will inspire reformers across the Middle East. And by helping Iraqis build a democracy, we will bring hope to a troubled region, and this will make America more secure in the long term.

This was consistent with Bush's style – the goal was ambitious, and the best response in the face of a setback was to become more entrenched. The only way the goals would not be achieved, Bush said, was if the US lost its nerve.[7]

Bush's commitment to staying in Iraq, as well as his approach to the interpersonal aspects of politics, was reflected in his embrace of the new Prime Minister Nuri al-Maliki. Maliki was a member of the Dawa party who had spent much of the Saddam era in exile under threat of death. Many in the US government were concerned that Maliki would favour the Shia, and be ineffective in dealing with Shiite militia. A leaked cable from National Security Advisor Stephen Hadley documented doubts about the Iraqi leader.

> We returned from Iraq convinced we need to determine if Prime Minister Maliki is both willing and able to rise above the sectarian agendas being promoted by others. Do we and Prime Minister Maliki share the same vision for Iraq? If so, is he able to curb those who seek Shia hegemony or the reassertion of Sunni power? […] Despite Maliki's reassuring words, repeated reports from our commanders on the ground contributed to our concerns about Maliki's government. Reports of nondelivery of services to Sunni areas, intervention by the prime minister's office to stop military action against Shia targets and to encourage them against Sunni ones, removal of Iraq's most effective commanders on a sectarian basis and efforts to ensure Shia majorities in all ministries — when combined with the escalation of Jaish al-Mahdi's (JAM) [the Arabic name for the Mahdi Army] killings — all suggest a campaign to consolidate Shia power in Baghdad.[8]

The president, though, preferred to bolster rather than challenge the Iraqi leader. 'You are my man,' he would say to Maliki.[9] A senior US official even counselled the president to be more restrained in his professions of support for Maliki during their regular video-conferences. Efforts to leverage Maliki into difficult choices could be undone by a presidential embrace, in much the same way that Paul Bremer had taken solace from Bush's cheerleading and concluded that he need not listen to others. 'Are you saying I'm the problem?' Bush asked the official.[10]

The result of the Samarra mosque bombing was a massive increase in the activities of Shiite militia, in particular their targeting of the Sunni. What had been a tenuous equilibrium – Shiites showing restraint in order to move the political process forward, hoping that the Sunni insurgency would wither away – collapsed. Iraq hovered on the brink of civil war. During this period, the president had reaffirmed his commitment to Iraq and to its new prime minister, whilst Rumsfeld had reaffirmed his belief that the goal should be to withdraw in an orderly fashion.

The inconsistency between the two approaches had been masked to this point by the lack of attention to detail from the president, the lack of any motivation for Rumsfeld to point out the divergence, and that fact that, prior to the mosque bombing and spike in violence, it had remained possible to construct a narrative that blended the approaches together: the Iraqi forces were growing stronger, the insurgency weaker, and so withdrawal and stability were being achieved simultaneously. After the mosque bombing, with sectarian violence rapidly escalating, the contradictions between the approaches to Iraq of Bush and Rumsfeld became undeniable.

President Bush could either change his goals in Iraq, or change his strategy. Over the summer and autumn of 2006, a public debate on the war, and a private debate within the administration, ensued. I first address the public debate, which leaned strongly toward withdrawal. The chapter then examines Rumsfeld's final arguments in favour of continuing his approach, and the circumstances of Bush's removal of his secretary of defence. I then address the post-Rumsfeld debate within the administration, which Bush ensured included consideration of sending more troops. It is important to understand both the domestic political context and the range of options considered publicly and privately in order to isolate the influence of Bush on the decision to surge, a topic which closes the chapter.

The public debate

Three options dominated the public debate about what should be done in Iraq after the Samarra bombing: an immediate withdrawal, a partition that would embrace rather than resist Iraqi sectarian divisions, and an accelerated process of transitioning security responsibility to the Iraqis.

First: a withdrawal as soon as was logistically possible. The emergence of this option as a viable part of the public debate came as something of a shock to the White House, which to this point had considered it the province of leftist extremists. Democrats looking ahead to the 2008 presidential primaries, competing for the support of the party base in the early primary states, begin to feel the allure of running on an immediate pullout. Hillary Clinton, whom the White House had judged to be responsible and moderate on Iraq policy and who was in some ways the president's favoured successor, was pulled to the left by the emergence of Senator Barack Obama, the only serious candidate for the Democratic nomination who had opposed the war from the outset. Obama's plan called for the removal of all troops by the end of 2008.

The second option that gained public attention was a partition of Iraq. Proponents of this sought to make a virtue of the divisions between Sunnis, Shiites and Kurds by giving substantial autonomy to these groups with a relatively weak central government in Baghdad. The plan, which relied heavily on an analogy between the situation in the former Yugoslavia in the 1990s and post-invasion Iraq, was first proposed by Chairmen of the Council on Foreign Relations Leslie Gelb in November 2003. Peter W. Galbraith, the former US Ambassador to Croatia, elaborated his own version in May 2004, and the plan received renewed attention in July 2006 when Senator Joseph Biden, the ranking Democrat and soon-to-be chair of the Senate Foreign Relations Committee, co-authored a *New York Times* op-ed with Gelb advocating the idea.[11] Biden argued that the Bush administration had no plan on Iraq other than leaving the war to the president's successor. Partition, Biden argued, was the only new and viable strategy on offer.[12]

Third, and most serious, was the array of recommendations in the final report of the Iraq Study Group (ISG). The ISG had been conducting an independent review of Iraq strategy since late 2005, holding hearings, interviewing experts and journeying to the country. It had been initially set up by the Bush administration as a public relations exercise. The administration had believed that progress was being made, but that the public debate was still focused on the mistakes of the CPA period. The solution, then, was to inaugurate a commission of distinguished Americans to observe in depth the situation in Iraq, then report back in a manner that would shift the public debate. Peter Feaver of the NSC explained to me that initially the administration was supportive of the ISG. It was composed of

> People like Vernon Jordan and Justice [Sandra Day] O'Conner. Notable, eminent Americans, but not national security experts or military strategists. They were the kind of people who would go to Iraq, and if they told Americans what's what, Americans would believe them. That was the theory, but in the interval between when that got launched and when it was time for them to report, the situation had changed in Iraq.[13]

The final ISG report began with a rejection of the president's talk of victory: 'The situation in Iraq is grave and deteriorating. There is no path that can guarantee success.'[14] The report went on to recommend some new initiatives – leaning harder on the Iraqis to make political progress, a re-engagement of some kind with the Israel-Palestine peace process, a 'diplomatic offensive' to persuade Iran, Syria and others to help the US calm the situation in Iraq. On the major issue – what to do with US forces – the recommendation was to quicken the transition to Iraqi responsibility for security and to withdraw US troops from the front lines: 'By the first quarter of 2008, subject to unexpected developments in the security situation on the ground, all combat brigades not necessary for force protection could be out of Iraq.'[15] The ISG report, then, was closer to Rumsfeld's view of the situation than to the president's.

Public opinion ran 2–1 in favour of the ISG recommendations, with a plurality in favour even among Republicans.[16] On the question of withdrawing troops by 2008, the split was stark: 71% in favour, only 26% opposed. The public overwhelmingly agreed with the ISG's rejection of Bush's talk of victory, with only 9% believing the war was likely to end this way and 87% judging a compromise settlement to be more likely.[17]

The president's overall handling of the war was harshly judged at this point. Polls just prior to the November 2006 congressional midterm elections showed only 29% approving of Bush's handling of the war, and an overall presidential approval rating of 34%.[18] The Congress, particularly after Democrats picked up thirty-one House and six Senate seats in the November elections in what was widely seen as a referendum on the handling of Iraq, was a source of constant criticism. On being elected speaker of the new House, Nancy Pelosi identified 'ending the war in Iraq' as her first priority, and said that the president could not expect a 'blank check' from the Congress to continue funding of the war.[19] Centrist Republicans had also turned against the president's handling of the war. In the Senate, the outgoing leader of the Foreign Relations Committee, Republican Richard Lugar, called for the administration to take its cue from Congress, which he suggested should hold a 'retreat' in order to determine Iraq strategy.[20]

The domestic political context, then, was that the Iraq war was seen as essentially lost, with orderly withdrawal seen as the best possible resolution. President Bush saw this as unacceptable, and so began to search for alternatives that would preserve the chance of victory.

Removing Rumsfeld

In order for the administration to have a serious debate about what to do in Iraq, Bush realized that Rumsfeld had to be removed. Rumsfeld was so personally associated with the withdrawal approach that a change of defence secretary had to be made before the strategy could be revised.

The president called a news conference to announce Rumsfeld's resignation on the day after the Democratic congressional election victory. He praised the secretary's service, the innovative nature of Rumsfeld's war plan in Iraq, and Rumsfeld's focus on transformation of the armed forces. Bush stated that Rumsfeld's replacement, Robert Gates, would provide 'a fresh perspective and new ideas on how America can achieve our goals in Iraq'.[21] Rumsfeld's comments that day emphasized the complexity of the situation in Iraq. It was 'a little understood, unfamiliar war, the first war of the twenty-first century – it is not well known, it is not well understood, it is complex for people to understand'.[22]

Both Bush and Rumsfeld have remained relatively quiet about the back-story of the resignation. Bush prized loyalty and sought to be decent towards those he had to remove from office, whilst Rumsfeld had little incentive to say much on the subject. One administration insider revealed, off-the-record, that former President George H.W. Bush had been very clear with his son that it was time for a change of secretary of defence.[23] Robert Gates, the new secretary, was a close associate of the former president and had served as director of the Central Intelligence Agency during the George H.W. Bush years.

In one of his few comments on the decision, Bush told Bob Woodward that 'as you begin to think new, it's more than just new strategy. It is new personnel... I was beginning to smell the problem politically at home'. Bush continued. 'The politics of the moment, obviously, wasn't driving me, because of the strategic implications of this. On the other hand, I also knew that the president's got to work hard to give people a sense of hope in the mission... Part of making sure the change of strategy became a change in people's minds was to also change some of the players, some of the personnel.'[24]

The president had decided in late summer 2006 that Rumsfeld had to be removed.[25] The decision process bore Bush's hallmarks. Although several of his advisors had previously suggested replacing Rumsfeld, including Chief of Staff Andrew Card on two occasions, Bush had at first refused to take the advice. In April 2006, several retired generals had taken the unusual step of calling for a sitting defence secretary to resign, and this had triggered Bush's stubbornness and his feelings of loyalty.[26] Card's replacement as chief of staff, Joshua Bolten, had also believed it was time for a change, but it took several months to convince Bush. When the president finally concluded that he needed a new secretary of defence, he characteristically had to ensure that he would feel personally comfortable with Rumsfeld's replacement.[27]

Rumsfeld's removal had been preceded by a summer in which the president had begun to challenge the existing approach to Iraq. As Peter Feaver, the NSC official, confirms:

> There [was] a logic behind Rumsfeld's position, and in the decades long view… it'll be the Iraqis who win this, not us. All those things which are core elements of the Rumsfeld approach are still true. The problem was the security challenge they were confronting was too big for them. They were going to not only fall off the bicycle but fall off the cliff. We had to reverse that security spiral before we could go back to Rumsfeld's plan.[28]

During the period following the Samarra Mosque bombing, Rumsfeld had shown diffidence toward Iraq policy. He had sought to disentangle himself and his department from much of the Iraq portfolio. Rumsfeld did not believe – as Bush did – that the level of violence was a reasonable metric of success in Iraq. He wrote down his thoughts on the issue in September 2006:

'The measures of success in Iraq have to be:
1. The size and success of the Iraqi Security Forces.
2. The number of provinces turned over.
3. The economic progress.
4. The political progress on reconciliation and the like.
5. Not the level of violence – that is controlled by the enemy. We have never lost even a platoon.'[29]

Whereas Bush had reduced the situation to its starkest essentials, Rumsfeld remained in thrall to the complexities. Would more troops make a difference? How could the strategy be better calibrated? In a meeting with defence analysts, Rumsfeld said 'there's no guidebook. You don't get taught this stuff in war college. This is tough stuff. It's an art. It isn't a science.'[30]

Bush directly challenged a central tenet of Rumsfeld's approach in a White House meeting on 17 August. When General Casey reported on the ability of Iraqi security forces to secure neighbourhoods, Bush said 'If they can't do it, we will. If the bicycle teeters, we're going to put the hand back on. We have to make damn sure they cannot fail.'[31] The schism between Bush and Rumsfeld was now clear and wide, although this remains one of the few times it was stated so openly by either party.

Yet Rumsfeld still did not abandon his approach. One month after the August meeting, the retired General Jack Keane visited him. Keane was a proponent of sending more troops to Iraq rather than continuing to withdraw. The General critiqued the Casey/Rumsfeld plan as

A defensive strategy. It relies heavily on establishing an effective government, enfran-
chising the Sunnis, isolating the insurgents, and bringing them into the political
process. There is plenty of logic to it – I thought it made some sense and believed in it
as did many others. But it is flawed and fundamentally so, in the view of what we know
now.[32]

Keane told Rumsfeld that the strategy he had crafted with General Casey seemed
'designed to get us out of there as quickly as possible' rather than defeat the insurgency. Keane proposed his preferred alternative: switch to a counter-insurgency
approach and send more troops. Rumsfeld, in accordance with his style, did not say
no outright, but instead asked questions: where will we get the additional troops
from? Why would more troops be decisive? But Keane could tell that Rumsfeld did
not agree with the argument that more troops would help.[33]

In addition to his reluctance to commit more forces, Rumsfeld was also deeply
influenced by the fact that his top generals did not support a change in strategy.
From Rumsfeld's combatant commanders, '[a]ll the pressure was downward on
the force levels – Abizaid, Casey, Franks – and that was a credible point of view
that Rumsfeld happened to share: keep the forces levels down, it'll put pressure
on the Iraqis to step up, to develop their own security forces, if we come in and
do this for them we'll never get out of here.'[34] When Keane proposed the replacement of Abizaid and Casey, Rumsfeld shot back 'These are very good men. They've
sacrificed.'[35]

Lawrence Di Rita stresses that this was a key factor for Rumsfeld:

> Rumsfeld found himself in a very unusual position on the surge. He was a big believer
> that you can't operate outside of the chain of command, and the body of the chain of
> command was rejecting the surge idea. So he found himself in a tough situation by virtue
> of Jack [Keane] coming in with a plan and the NSC [also generating an alternative].
> So Rumsfeld found himself in a position of having to impose something on the mili-
> tary chain of command or just get out of the way and let the president make the changes
> needed to get new leadership...including military leadership..and fresh eyes on the
> situation.[36]

Two days prior to his departure, Rumsfeld sent to the White House a hastily
composed memo on 'illustrative new courses of action' in Iraq. The document was
not intended to be 'prescriptive or definitive, but he hoped it would at least provoke
further debate'.[37] Di Rita reports that Rumsfeld saw it as 'trying to clear the decks, to
make it easy for the president to say "this makes sense...this is the classic Rumsfeld
let's get all the options on the table", knowing full well that he was not going to be
the one to [implement them]'.[38]

This memo, the motivation for which may always be open to debate given its
timing (was it just for posterity?), stated boldly that 'In my view it is time for a
major adjustment. Clearly, what US forces are currently doing in Iraq is not working

well enough or fast enough.' In customary Rumsfeld style, the secretary was ellip-
tical about his own preferences, laying out twenty-one options and innovations
that could be tried, many 'in combination with others'. These were divided into
'above the line' attractive options, and 'below the line' less attractive choices. Many
of the 'above the line' options were re-endorsements or accelerations of the existing strategy. What would become the president's new approach – 'Increase Brigade
Combat Teams and US forces in Iraq substantially' – was a 'below the line' option
for Rumsfeld.[39] The thrust of the memo was that the Iraqis had to do more and do
it more quickly.

Rumsfeld, then, left the administration without having changed his view on what
was appropriate in Iraq. In a revealing *Fox News* interview after his successor Robert
Gates had been confirmed, Rumsfeld said

> If there is a ditch to be dug, an American does not want to sit down and teach an Iraqi
> how to dig that ditch. He will – he'll go dig the dad-burned ditch. It'll be a beautiful
> ditch. But that is not what the task is. The task is to get the Iraqis to dig the ditches. And
> I use that figuratively, obviously. So you – on the one hand, you don't want to feed the
> insurgency. On the other hand, you don't want to create a dependency. So at some point,
> you've got to take your hand off the bicycle seat. You get the bicycle running down the
> middle of the street with your youngster on it, and you're pushing and you're holding it
> up, and you know if you let go – you go from a full hand to three fingers to two fingers to
> one finger, and you know if you let go, they might fall. You also know if you don't let go,
> you're going to end up with a 40-year-old that can't ride a bike. Now, that's not a happy
> prospect.[40]

This was an encapsulation of Rumsfeld's view on prosecuting the war, and the president had now rejected it.

Surge decision process

With Rumsfeld removed, the administration considered options that would achieve
Bush's goals. Whilst it was important that all options be considered, Bush had made
it clear, by his statements and his firing of Rumsfeld, that the status quo was not
acceptable. It is important to understand the range of options under consideration
within the government so that we can trace the impact of Bush's individual characteristics on the choice of the surge.

Bush ordered the agencies of national security to conduct reviews of the war
strategy. The Joint Chiefs of Staff convened a 'Colonels Committee', including the
iconoclast hero of Tal Afar H.R. McMaster. This committee came up with three main
options: Go Big – add more troops; Go Long – withdraw US forces from combat
roles and embed advisors in Iraqi units to stiffen them; or Get Out. The JCS deliberations were hampered by conflicting imperatives. While no general officer wanted

to leave Iraq with the job half-done, the armed forces command was concerned that the military could not cope with the strain of deployment at current force levels. 'Go Long' was their preference.[41] Pete Schoomaker, the army chief of staff, told Congress in testimony on 13 December that the army 'will break' if the pressure of current commitments was not relieved.[42] General Casey himself declined to reconsider his strategy. Peter Feaver says 'Casey didn't think the strategy was not working. He thought it could be tweaked, refined at the margins, but he thought basically we were still doing the right thing.'[43]

The State Department's review process was inconclusive, largely due to the tortured ruminations of the secretary of state herself. Bing West writes that 'Condoleezza Rice, as the national security adviser, glossed over the basic contradiction between the White House and the Pentagon in 2003 and 2004. Then, as secretary of state in 2005, she endorsed a military strategy of clear and hold, opposing the Pentagon strategy of standing up Iraqi forces and leaving.'[44] When Casey announced his intention to continue a drawdown, she became furious with the drawdown of troops, erupting at news in June 2006 of the withdrawal of a combat brigade.[45] However, West continues, 'In late 2006, she again reversed course in favor of declaring victory and leaving.'[46]

Rice's top aides on Iraq, Philip Zelikow and David Satterfield, drafted a memo that reflected her latest views. The original objectives in Iraq had been 'substantially accomplished' and future steps were for the Iraqis themselves to decide upon, within the context of a 'more arms length' US-Iraq relationship.[47] The ambassador to Iraq, Zalmay Khalilzad, argued that more troops were not the answer, and concurred with the notion of scaling back direct US involvement. 'Proposals to send more US forces to Iraq would not produce a long-term solution and would make our policy less, not more, sustainable', he wrote from Baghdad.[48]

Members of a small, energetic group in the NSC felt that they had a viable alternative.[49] This group thought the State option defeatist and one Bush would not agree to, and Rumsfeld's approach was seen as 'temporizing'.[50] Meghan O'Sullivan, J.D. Crouch, Peter Feaver and Brett McGurk called themselves the 'surgios', and were keen to make sure the president had the option to add more troops in a targeted way. The surgios thought more troops could make a difference if they were focused on securing Baghdad and embraced classic counter-insurgency principles.

The NSC staff ensured that the president heard from a range of outside experts – Jack Keane, whose discussions with Rumsfeld were detailed above, Frederick Kagan of the American Enterprise Institute, who had been working on the details of how additional troops might change the course of the war, Eliot Cohen of Johns Hopkins University, who stressed the importance of getting the right military leadership in place, and Stephen Biddle, a Brookings Institution strategist skilled at cutting to the core of strategic choices. This group met with Bush once in June, when the president was not yet at the point of being willing to change course, and again, with more consequence, in December.

The interagency review concluded on 26 November with Deputy National Security Advisor J.D. Crouch presenting a summary to the president. Crouch told Bush that there was most support for an accelerated version of the Rumsfeld/Casey plan, with a minority report in favour of a surge. Rice argued for stepping back from Iraq to 'create leverage', while Pace stated that the sectarian violence was now so bad in Iraq that it may not be possible for the military to quell it.[51]

In a 9 December NSC session Bush announced a key principle for moving forward: US troops in Baghdad could not remain passive in the face of the sectarian violence. No political progress was possible until the levels of violence were under control. This signalled the death of the Rumsfeld/Casey plan. On 11 December, the NSC staff arranged for a new meeting between the president and Keane, Kagan, Cohen and Biddle. There is good evidence that this meeting represented the culmination of Bush's decision process.[52]

Bush had recently visited Iraqi Prime Minister Maliki and reaffirmed his confidence in his motives and abilities, and so, prior to the second meeting of the outside experts, many of the elements of the surge decision were in place. At this second meeting, everyone was direct – the group told Bush that the situation was dire and his handling of the war thus far had been 'dismal'.[53] 'I was a lot blunter than I'd been in June' in calling for a change of strategy and a change of commanding general, remembers Eliot Cohen. 'I said we keep talking of the generals as great guys, and so and so is a great guy, and I said that's not important. What's important is: are they successful guys?'[54] General Keane told Bush that there was a crisis in Iraq, time was against him, and the surge option was the only one that had a chance of working quickly enough to rescue the situation.[55]

The major hurdle in finally convincing the president, others recall, was in making him comfortable with rejecting the advice of the military command, a move that cut against his preference to delegate and his collegial approach to interpersonal relations. 'The president wasn't sure how to go about picking Generals,' says Stephen Biddle. 'He was fairly comfortable relying on the military's corporate expertise on a lot of things, including picking people.'[56] Here, the availability of General David Petraeus, one of the few commanders of sufficient stature with an excellent combat record in Iraq, and also a forward thinker on counter-insurgency with support among the NSC staff, was crucial.

Bush then went over to the Pentagon for a difficult meeting with the joint chiefs, and told them that while he was concerned about force over-stretch, victory in Iraq had to take priority. There were few things Bush cared about more than the health of the US military, he said, but losing in Iraq was one of them.[57] On 15 December, in an NSC meeting, the president announced his decision to the principals by way of a summary of how he viewed the options: 'We can hold steady. None of you say it's working. We can redeploy for failure – that's your option, Condi. Or we can surge for success.'[58]

Bush and the surge

Bush's worldview and leadership style were critical to the choice of the surge strategy. An individual with a different personality and style would not have chosen the surge option. The remainder of the chapter links Bush's individual characteristics to the surge choice.

Closed-mindedness and delegation

A criticism that can fairly be levelled against the president is that his closed-minded style delayed the strategy shift. As earlier chapters have shown, the basic divergence between the Bush and Rumsfeld approaches to Iraq was apparent from the first days of the conflict, but the president did not insist on the approach matching his goals until very late in the course of the war.

Bush accepted too readily and for too long the assurances of, in particular, Secretary Rumsfeld, the Joint Chiefs, and the theatre commander that the existing 'they stand up/we stand down' approach was working. An incredible amount of information as to the inadequacy of the existing approach was necessary before Bush gave serious thought to a shift in strategy. Even the strongest defenders of the president, such as Peter Wehner, the former director of the White House Office of Strategic Initiatives, acknowledge that the change 'happened later than it should have. The president's disposition is certainly to defer to the judgment of the military, and he did. But he did for too long'.[59]

Philip Zelikow felt that Bush had accepted having the theatre commander and CENTCOM chief – Abizaid and Casey – play an outsized role in deciding strategy. The White House was 'looking to Baghdad to not just execute the strategy, but to write the strategy and to form the policy and then to tell Washington'. The dynamic, then, was 'Baghdad briefs, Washington listens'.[60] Thomas Ricks reported that when the president, prior to late 2006, was told he was not winning the war, 'He didn't want to hear it' and 'tended not to believe it'.[61]

Bush's preference for delegation and for the avoidance of interpersonal conflict, then, was a major cause of the delay in changing course. Representative Rob Simmons of Connecticut, brought in for a meeting with the president with about twenty other Republican House members, confronted him directly on this point: 'I suggested to him that he needed to be more involved in the strategic policy with regard to Iraq and terrorism, and he said "I'm not going to be like President Johnson, sitting around a map picking bombing targets"... we had an interesting interaction.' Simmons felt Bush was too willing to accept easy reassurances from his generals and not interested enough in probing more deeply: 'He treats his generals as if they are division heads. "Okay, we've got Casey, we've got whomever, this is their responsibility".'[62]

When it comes to the generals, Michael Gordon of the *New York Times* concurs, Bush was 'in receive mode'.[63] Retired General Jack Keane, one of those the NSC brought in to meet with Bush during this period, wonders to what extent the president, prior to late 2006, fully understood how the Rumsfeld/Casey plan translated to on-the-ground operations: '[H]ere's the reason why I pose the question: Because the rhetoric that the president was evidencing in his remarks almost consistently for three years, he would use terms like "win"; "we're going to defeat the insurgents"; "victory". That all would lend itself to a military strategy whose purpose was to defeat the insurgency. We never had that as a mission in Iraq.' With the focus on transitioning to Iraqis and drawing back US troops to Forward Operating Bases, there had been no 'forcing function' in the US plan.[64]

Black-and-white worldview, radical shift in strategy

As is often the case in individuals with black-and-white worldviews, once the inflection point is reached, the change in approach is wholesale and fundamental rather than incremental and peripheral. Choosing the surge required rejection of the assumptions under which US policy in Iraq had operated since March 2003.[65]

Bush conceptualized the Iraq war in terms of victory and defeat. Nuanced, compromise solutions did not form a part of his worldview. In the circumstances of the Iraq strategy review, this translated into a stubborn refusal to admit defeat and accept retreat. Only the surge option satisfied the core goals of the president.

As Peter Wehner puts it, 'the acid test on these things is always whether they work or not. If you take a stand, against opposition, and you're right, you look principled and courageous and admirable. If you take a stand that's unpopular and wrong, you look stubborn and foolish, rigid and inflexible.'[66] Thomas Donnelly of the American Enterprise Institute (AEI) concurs: 'any rehabilitation of Bush's reputation will be rooted in his alleged "state of denial" – which is to say, his unwillingness to accept defeat'.[67]

In a televised exit interview, Bush was asked to reflect upon a moment across his two terms in office when he had thought 'If I do that, I'll be compromising on principle'. Without hesitation, Bush nominated:

> The pullout of Iraq. It would have compromised the principle that when you put kids into harm's way, you go in to win. And it was a tough call, particularly since a lot of people were advising for me to get out of Iraq, or pull back in Iraq … I listened to a lot of voices, but ultimately I listened to this voice: I'm not going to let your son die in vain, I believe we can win; I'm going to do what it takes to win in Iraq.[68]

President Bush's worldview determined that many options in Iraq would be unacceptable to him. In particular, the option of withdrawal, as suggested by the Iraq Study Group, was not going to be selected by Bush. As Lee Hamilton, co-chair of the ISG, put it: 'Bush was very gracious, said we've worked hard and did this great service for the country – and he ignored it [the report] so far as I can see. He fundamentally didn't agree with it. President Bush has always sought … a victory, a military victory. And we did not recommend that. The gist of what we had to say was a responsible exit. He didn't like that.'[69]

Former Secretary of Defence William Perry felt that when Bush himself talked to the ISG as part of their deliberations:

> He was not seeking advice from us, he was telling us what his view of the war was … It was a Churchillian kind of a thing … There's going to be blood, sweat, and tears and all that. It was that sort of a moment. It is quite clear that he had this image of a great global struggle, and he was presiding over it, and Iraq was just one element of that, and that the people who were wavering on Iraq did not see the big picture the way he saw it.[70]

Frederick Kagan of AEI felt that the overall effect of the ISG had been to demonstrate that the only middle course that existed in Iraq was a slightly slower defeat than immediate withdrawal and – 'knowing the president at all', Bush was 'not going to leave'.[71] Stephen Biddle, the defence expert who was a key figure in the December White House meetings, had long felt that middle-ground temporizing was not an intellectually or strategically coherent policy:

> My position throughout, and my position in the White House meeting was 'one or the other.' But the President wasn't remotely interested in getting out. So to make an argument that it was one or the other, in that setting, meant that it was the one. It was obvious that it would be pointless to argue for cutting our losses and getting out. He just wasn't going to accept that.[72]

Indeed, for all the careful construction of an array of options involving various timetables, mechanisms and devices, Bush's angular mind reduced the final decision calculus to just two stark choices, as he told Bob Woodward: 'One [option] was kind of pull out of Baghdad and if it burnt down, so be it, as long as it doesn't spread. And the other was get in there and get after it and make it work. And I obviously chose the latter.'[73]

The president played a role in the generation of options during this period, becoming involved in the policy process at an earlier stage than he had in other Iraq war decisions. Bush addressed a meeting of the Joint Chiefs of Staff in late 2006, and, according to Michael Gordon of the *New York Times*, told them 'I'm not interested in hearing from you about withdrawal and how to get out. I'm interested in learning how we can win … tell me how we can succeed.' That's the message he sends to his own military.'[74] Bush knew that the leadership of the military was concerned about the strain on the force, but delivered what Fred Barnes termed a 'sharp rejoinder, touching on a theme he returned to in nearly every meeting on Iraq: "The biggest strain on the force would be a defeat in Iraq," he said'.[75] The army chief of staff, General Pete Schoomaker, had told Bush directly that he did not support a surge, and it probably wouldn't work, certainly not in the time Bush would get from the American public: 'Pete,' Bush replied, 'I'm the president, and I've got the time.'[76]

Bush had National Security Advisor Stephen Hadley ensure that options to send more troops were being considered in all of the post-Rumsfeld policy reviews.

Hadley said 'You have got to give the President the option of a surge in forces. You present him everything else you're talking about, but I'm telling you, you have got to give him that option of a surge in forces. He will want to see it.'[77]

History maker, risk acceptance

Finally, Bush's preference for a bold, history-making stance was important to the choice of the surge. There was audacity in the belief that the surge could succeed in altering the situation in Iraq. Having spurned the offer of bipartisan cover for a dignified withdrawal under the ISG plan, and facing a new Congress after the 2006 midterms where Democrats had made major gains on a platform of withdrawal from Iraq, the surge policy could have been strangled in the cradle by a congressional vote to mandate withdrawal.

As Bush announced the surge, the view in many quarters was that the Iraq war had become unwinnable. The ISG had labelled prospects of a positive outcome 'implausible'.[78] The US Institute for Peace had brought together twenty experts in late 2006 to think through the likely scenarios in Iraq. The results were sobering: 'positive outcomes would be hard to achieve, and negative outcomes could be foreseen much more easily.' The list of easily foreseen negative outcomes included 'Ethnic-Sectarian Politics Derail the Political Process'; 'Descent into Hell'; and 'Lebanonization'. 'Even the less negative scenarios … required some leaps of faith and careful coordinated cooperation of the many actors [involved].' 'The negative scenarios are not predicated on any surprising event or US blunder. Rather, they are based on forces the experts saw as inexorable at worst or unsurprising at best. The participants found it difficult to imagine effective and realistic countermeasures to avoid these kinds of negative outcomes.'[79]

Bush didn't need to rely on outside groups to indicate the scope of the risk he was taking: the director of national intelligence, John Negroponte, produced an official National Intelligence Estimate in January 2007 that was profoundly pessimistic. Given current US and Iraqi capabilities, the security situation looked likely to continue to deteriorate. Even if the security situation were to improve, 'given the current winner-take-all attitude and sectarian animosities infecting the political scene, Iraqi leaders will be hard pressed to achieve sustained political reconciliation.'[80]

Andrew Krepenivich, a defence expert, suggested that while securing Baghdad and then progressively pacifying the rest of the country was an 'attractive' idea, the risks were 'formidable'.[81] The retired Colonel Douglas MacGregor called it 'delusional thinking' and 'a prescription for getting a lot of Americans killed'.[82] In April 2007, as surge brigades continued to roll in, Democratic Senate leader Harry Reid called on Bush to acknowledge that 'the war is lost'.[83] In congressional testimony, Ambassador to Iraq Ryan Crocker said 'we are one car bomb away from utter devastation…There's a limit beyond which society just begins to come unglued'.[84] Derek Harvey of the Defence Intelligence Agency judged the chances of success at one in six, while Stephen Biddle, who had been involved in the process that led to making the decision, judged the odds of success at one in ten. Even Bush's new defence secretary, Robert Gates, who had been sounded out prior to being offered the post as to his views on a surge, was 'neutral, even dour, about the chances of success in Iraq'.[85] Philip Zelikow, Condoleezza Rice's advisor who was among the first in the administration to become disenchanted with the Rumsfeld/Casey plan, also felt the surge to be a gamble – the act of a stock market investor with all his money in one risky stock.[86]

Eliot Cohen and Stephen Biddle, two of the outside experts who advised Bush during this period, agreed in interviews that the surge decision has to be looked at in terms of Bush's risk acceptance. Cohen, a student of wartime leadership, suggests that 'not many political leaders would have had the guts to say "I'm going to double-down in Iraq." And, you know, courage and persistence count for a lot in wars. You've got to have brains and good judgment. But you know what? Courage and persistence will actually get you pretty far.'[87]

Asked directly about his public estimates of the 'long shot' nature of the surge, and about what the decision therefore tells us about Bush's propensity for risk-taking, Biddle said

> I'm on record during that period having assessed the odds of success as being in the ten to twenty percent range, so you can quote me on that. One will also recall from what I said that there are times at which ten to twenty percent long shots are the optimal strategy. Pursuant to your theme of was the president risk-acceptant: yes, absolutely. But you have to bear in mind that a ten-percent long shot looks an awful lot better when you think that all the alternatives are zero percent failures. Again, a lot of people in the debate were willing to contemplate complete withdrawal as a plausible alternative, and I said at the time and I still think looking back, that when you are looking at a ten-percent long shot, a complete withdrawal is a credible alternative. It wasn't a credible alternative to the president… he had ruled out the non-long-shot alternative.[88]

In the last big decision he made on Iraq, having finally resolved the conflict with Rumsfeld by removing the secretary, Bush's distinctive personality and decision style was indispensable to the choice he made. Bush's closed cognitive style and tendency to delegate was a key influence in delaying the strategy shift, his black-and-white worldview eliminated the options of rapid withdrawal, and his history-making temperament led him to be comfortable in selecting a strategy described to him as a gamble and a long shot.

Notes

1 This chapter is a revised and extended (especially on Rumsfeld) version of the argument in Stephen Benedict Dyson, 'George W. Bush, the Surge, and Presidential Leadership', *Political Science Quarterly* 125 (2010/11): 557–586.

2   Edward Wong, 'More Clashes Shake Iraq; Political Talks Are in Ruins', *New York Times*, 24 February 2006.

3   Figures for civilian deaths at www.iraqbodycount.org/database/, accessed 29 June 2009.

4   Author interview with Feaver.

5   Steven R. Weisman, 'Rumsfeld Learns to Curb His Enthusiasm', *New York Times*, 30 April 2006, 3.

6   Thom Shanker, 'Iraqi Forces Would Handle Any Civil War, Rumsfeld Says', *New York Times*, 10 March 2006.

7   David E. Sanger, 'Bush, Conceding Problems, Defends Iraq War', *New York Times*, 13 March 2006.

8   'Text of US Security Advisor's Memo', *New York Times*, 29 November 2006. Available at www.nytimes.com/2006/11/29/world/middleeast/29mtext.html.

9   Linda Robinson, *Tell Me How This Ends: General David Petraeus and the Search for a Way Out of Iraq* (New York: Public Affairs, 2009), 24.

10 Robinson, *Tell Me How This Ends*, 11.

11 Peter W. Galbraith, 'How to Get out of Iraq', *New York Review of Books*, 13 May 2004; Joseph R. Biden, Jr and Leslie H. Gelb, 'Unity through Autonomy in Iraq', *New York Times*, 1 July 2006, available at http://query.nytimes.com/gst/fullpage.html?res=9405EEDE113FF932 A35756C0A9609C8B63.

12 Joseph R. Biden, Jr, 'A Plan to Hold Iraq Together', *Washington Post*, 24 August 2006; p. A21.

13 Author interview with Feaver.

14 James A. Baker and Lee M. Hamilton, *The Iraq Study Group Report*, 6 December 2006, available at www.usip.org/isg/iraq_study_group_report/report/1206/iraq_study_group _report.pdf, 6.

15 Baker and Hamilton, *Iraq Study Group Report*, 7.

16 Newsweek Poll, 6–7 December 2006, available at www.pollingreport.com/iraq8.htm, accessed 8 July 2009.

17 Associated Press/Ipsos poll, 4–6 December 2006, available at www.pollingreport.com/ iraq8.htm.

18 New York Times/CBS Poll, 27–31 October 2006, available at http://graphics8.nytimes. com/packages/pdf/politics/20061031_poll.pdf.

19 Nancy Pelosi, 'Bringing the war to an end is my highest priority as speaker', available at www.huffingtonpost.com/rep-nancy-pelosi/bringing-the-war-to-an-en_b_34393.html, accessed 2 July 2009.

20 John Dunbar, 'Lugar: Bush, Congress should discuss war', *Associated Press*, 31 December 2006, available at www.sfgate.com/cgi-bin/article.cgi?f=/n/a/2006/12/31/national/ w083109S02.DTL&hw=Lugar&sn=001&sc=1000.

21 George W. Bush, 'Remarks on the Resignation of Secretary of Defense Donald H. Rumsfeld and the Nomination of Robert M. Gates to be Secretary of Defense', 8 November 2006. Available at www.presidency.ucsb.edu/ws/index.php?pid=24262&st=&st1=.

22 Thomas E. Ricks, *The Gamble* (New York: Penguin, 2009), 76.

23 Interview information.

24 Bob Woodward, *The War Within* (New York: Simon & Schuster, 2008), 196–197.

25 Jim Rutenberg, 'Removal of Rumsfeld Dates Back to the Summer', *New York Times*, 10 November 2006. Available at www.nytimes.com/2006/11/10/washington/10Rumsfeld. html.

26 Perry Bacon, Jr. 'The Revolt of the Generals', *Time*, 16 April 2006, available at www.time. com/time/magazine/article/0,9171,1184048,00.html.

27 Rutenberg, 'Removal of Rumsfeld Dates Back to the Summer'.

28 Author interview with Feaver.
29 Rumsfeld, 'Measures of Success in Iraq', 18 September 2006. http://library.Rumsfeld.com/doclib/sp/470/Re%20Measures%20of%20Success%20in%20Iraq%2009-18-2006.pdf.
30 Bradley Graham, *By His Own Rules: The Ambitions, Successes, and Ultimate Failures of Donald Rumsfeld* (New York: Public Affairs, 2009), 601.
31 Graham, *By His Own Rules*, 628–629.
32 Graham, *By His Own Rules*, 637
33 Graham, *By His Own Rules*, 638.
34 Author interview with Di Rita.
35 Graham, *By His Own Rules*, 639.
36 Author interview with Di Rita.
37 Graham, *By His Own Rules*, 651.
38 Author interview with Di Rita.
39 Donald Rumsfeld to George W. Bush, 'Iraq – Illustrative New Courses of Action', 6 November 2006. Available at www.nytimes.com/2006/12/03/world/middleeast/03mtext.html?pagewanted=print.
40 Interview with Secretary Donald Rumsfeld and Cal Thomas of Fox News Watch, 7 December 2006, available at www.defense.gov/transcripts/transcript.aspx?transcriptid=3824.
41 Robin Wright and Ann Scott Tyson, 'Joint Chiefs Advise Change in War Strategy', *Washington Post*, 14 December 2006, available at www.washingtonpost.com/wp-dyn/content/article/2006/12/13/AR2006121301379.html, accessed 2 July 2009.
42 Peter Baker, 'US Not Winning War in Iraq, Bush Says For First Time', *Washington Post*, 20 December 2006.
43 Author interview with Feaver.
44 Bing West, *The Strongest Tribe: War, Politics and the Endgame in Iraq* (New York: Random House, 2008), 362.
45 Bradley Graham, 'Exit Strategy: The Final Days of Donald Rumsfeld', *Washington Post*, 12 June 2009.
46 West, *The Strongest Tribe*, 362.
47 Woodward, *The War Within*, 232–233.
48 Michael R. Gordon, 'Troop Surge Took Place amid Doubt and Debate', *New York Times*, 31 August 2008, available at www.nytimes.com/2008/08/31/washington/31military.html?_r=1&ref=world&pagewanted=print, accessed 30 June 2009.
49 Excellent insight on the narrative of the surge decision, and its importance for debates on civil-military relations, has been provided by one of these senior staffers: Peter D. Feaver, who was at the time on secondment from Duke University. See Peter D. Feaver, 'Anatomy of the Surge', *Weekly Standard*, 4–28 April 2008, and Peter D. Feaver, 'The Right to be Right: Civil-Military Relations and the Iraq Surge Decision', *International Security* 35 (2011), 87–125.
50 West, *The Strongest Tribe*, 204.
51 Woodward, *The War Within*, 245.
52 This is Thomas Ricks' judgement in *The Gamble*, 95.
53 Michael A. Fletcher and Thomas E. Ricks, 'Experts Advise Bush Not to Reduce Troops', *Washington Post*, 12 December 2006, available at www.washingtonpost.com/wp-dyn/content/article/2006/12/11/AR2006121100508_pf.html.
54 Author interview with Eliot A. Cohen, 19 February 2009, Washington, DC.
55 *PBS Frontline*, Interview with General Jack Keane, 8 February 2007 and 1 May 2007, available at www.pbs.org/wgbh/pages/frontline/endgame/interviews/keane.html.
56 Author interview with Stephen Biddle, 10 March 2009, by telephone.

57 Steve Coll, 'The General's Dilemma', available at www.newamerica.net/publications/articles/2008/generals_dilemma_7865, accessed 1 July 2009; also Feaver, 'The Right to be Right', 8.

58 Woodward, *The War Within*, 292.

59 Author interview with Wehner.

60 *PBS Frontline*, Interview with Zelikow.

61 *PBS Frontline*, Interview with Ricks.

62 Author interview with Congressman Rob Simmons, 20 October 2008, Storrs, CT.

63 *PBS Frontline*, Interview with Gordon.

64 *PBS Frontline*, Interview with Keane.

65 National Security Council, 'Highlights of the Iraq Strategy Review, January 2007, Summary briefing Slides', available at: http://georgewbush-whitehouse.archives.gov/nsc/iraq/2007/iraq-strategy011007.pdf.

66 Author interview with Wehner.

67 Thomas Donnelly, 'Lincoln, Churchill, Bush?' Available at www.aei.org/article/29071.

68 ABC News, 'Charlie Gibson interviews President Bush', 1 December 2008, available at http://abcnews.go.com/WN/Politics/story?id=6356046&page=1.

69 Cullen Murphy and Todd S. Purdum, 'Farewell to All That: An Oral History of the Bush White House', available at www.vanityfair.com/politics/features/2009/02/bush-oral-history200902.

70 Woodward, *The War Within*, 214.

71 *PBS Frontline*, Interview with Kagan.

72 Author interview with Biddle.

73 Woodward, *The War Within*, 269.

74 *PBS Frontline*, Interview with Gordon.

75 Fred Barnes, 'How Bush Decided on the Surge', *The Weekly Standard*, 4 February 2008, available at www.weeklystandard.com/Content/Public/Articles/000/000/014/658dwgrn.asp.

76 Woodward, *The War Within*, 288.

77 Woodward, *The War Within*, 235.

78 Baker and Hamilton, *Iraq Study Group Report*, 29.

79 Alan Schwartz, '*Scenarios for the Insurgency in Iraq*', United States Institute of Peace Special Report no. 174, October 2006, available at www.usip.org/pubs/specialreports/sr174.pdf, 1, 9.

80 Office of the Director of National Intelligence, '*Prospects for Iraq's Stability: A Challenging Road Ahead*', available at www.dni.gov/press_releases/20070202_release.pdf.

81 *PBS Frontline*, Interview with Krepinevich.

82 *PBS Frontline*, Interview with Col. Douglas MacGregor, available at www.pbs.org/wgbh/pages/frontline/endgame/themes/casey.html#macgregor.

83 Associated Press, 'Reid: Iraq War Lost: US Can't Win', 20 April 2007, available at www.msnbc.msn.com/id/18227928/.

84 Robinson, *Tell Me How This Ends*, 151.

85 West, *The Strongest Tribe*, 272.

86 Woodward, *The War Within*, 317.

87 Author interview with Cohen.

88 Author interview with Biddle.

9

Leadership and the Iraq war – Lessons learned

George W. Bush's worldview was based upon clear-cut principles, instinctive, non-reflective decision making, a strong moralistic bent, and a propensity for risk-taking based upon a belief in the history-making potential of strong leadership. His administrative style, though, was delegatory and based upon maintaining comity. He preferred reading people to reading policy papers.

Donald H. Rumsfeld was, in many ways, the opposite of the president he served. Rumsfeld saw the world as filled with nuance, complexity and contingency. He was obsessed with the unknowable, and deeply suspicious of grand doctrines or ambitious policy schemes. His administrative style was actively conflict-seeking and involved the relentless challenge of the assumptions of others.

The interaction of these styles shaped every stage of the Iraq conflict. The shock of 9/11 motivated President Bush to focus intently upon foreign policy. He was drawn to a stark framing of the post-9/11 world as a battle between good and evil. His history-making bent drew him toward an ambitious and proactive response, and moralism combined with ambition in a deeply held commitment to the promotion of democracy. The Bush doctrine, then, was well named: another individual in the position of president following 9/11 would have responded to the events differently.

Donald Rumsfeld favoured a different strategic response. He disliked doctrines in general and the Bush variant in particular. He sought to prevent the declaration of a war on terror, troubled by its inaccurate presupposing of an entirely military response and its connotations of vengeance and punishment. He was not interested in the promotion of democracy abroad.

The invasion planning for Iraq, though, did fully engage his attention. Rumsfeld's preference for an iterative process, precise written work and the elaboration of fundamental assumptions and uncertainties was well suited to the war planning task. He was fortunate to find, in Gen. Tommy Franks, a partner who understood how best to respond to his aggressive questioning. Together, they fashioned a sleek plan that was devastatingly effective.

Things went awry in planning for developments after the invasion. The governance of a defeated foreign state, while highly relevant to Bush's goals of democracy promotion, was not at all part of Rumsfeld's concept of worthy uses of US power. He hoped an adequate solution could be found in the idea of a rolling transfer of authority to Iraqis, but was not committed to the idea and vacillated on the topic, mostly just seeking to avoid involvement. This, of course, was self-defeating, as the actions of L. Paul Bremer – who did not respond well to the secretary's management style – embroiled the US in exactly the type of nation-building operations that Rumsfeld thought unwise.

President Bush's leadership during this post-invasion phase was also subpar. Delegating the achievement of the goal of democratization to officials who disagreed with it (Rumsfeld) or had an idiosyncratic view of how to do it (Bremer) proved highly problematic. For more than three years, a leader capable of great clarity and a remarkable steadfastness allowed his central policy to descend into drift, chaos and near failure. The interaction of his incurious acceptance of what he was being told, disinterest in details and tendency to delegate brought him to the brink of defeat on the issue that mattered to him most.

At the last possible moment, Bush awakened. The decision to surge troops into Iraq showed the most resolute facets of his leadership. The issue was clear-cut: defeat or victory. Bush showed a willingness to embrace risk in pursuit of an ambitious goal, rejecting the counsels of caution that surrounded him. The delegatory style was put aside in favour of exercising decisive – many would say stubborn and wilful – leadership.

This was the end of the road for Rumsfeld, and the parting of the ways was a necessary element of Bush taking charge of the war. Rumsfeld was not enamoured of the idea of the US military solving Iraq's problems. If the Iraqi leadership was so weak – or its people so hateful of one another – that they were willing to have a civil war, then that was regrettable but its prevention was not a fundamental US policy interest. It was not worth further expenditure of money and lives, and the more the US increased its involvement, the less likely the problem would be solved. Iraqis would free-ride on US efforts, whilst the presence of US forces was itself an incitement to violence. Better, Rumsfeld thought, to withdraw and let the Iraqis get on with it.

Tables 9.1 and 9.2 offer an overview of the argument, illustrating where the personalities of Bush and Rumsfeld were most influential in Iraq decision making. This overview is not, of course, a substitute for the detail and context provided in the earlier chapters, but should act to draw the argument together.

What have we learned from the study of these two leaders in this defining early twenty-first-century conflict? First, and most obviously, that leadership itself matters. The choice for war, and the course of post-Saddam Iraq, was shaped by the worldviews and administrative styles of the US president and the secretary of defence. Other individuals occupying these roles, faced with the same situations, would have made different choices. Individuals shaped the history of the war. While historians and scholars of the presidency, for example, may find it axiomatic that personality is important to political outcomes, this core point does bear emphasis given the circumscribed role individual variables are afforded in many political science explanations of international relations and foreign policy.

Second, each configuration of style and worldview has advantages and disadvantages. The assumption in much of the literature on leadership is that some types of leaders are better than others. Open-minded and highly engaged leaders, running collegial and inclusive advisory systems, seem to be the preference.[1] It is the interaction between a leader's style and their circumstances that holds the key to success, however. Leadership is only part of the equation producing policy, and it follows then that the key driver of success is not the leader's style considered in isolation but rather the fit between leader and circumstance.

In the circumstances of the surge decision, George W. Bush's stubbornness and definitive mindset led him to a policy choice that was opposed by those around him and the wider public, was extremely risky, yet produced a better outcome than the other available options. In the circumstances of invasion planning, Rumsfeld's relentless questioning of basic assumptions, stress on the unknowability of the future and interrogatory interpersonal style drove General Tommy Franks toward an innovative and highly successful plan. Later, though, the interaction of Bush's hands-off, cheerleading interpersonal style and Rumsfeld's idiosyncratic approach to the management of L. Paul Bremer drove post-war policy in a strange direction.

Students of leadership, then, should be cautious in lauding certain traits of style and personality and deprecating others. Rather than there being an ideal type or style for high office, it is more the case that each style has virtues and vices. The range of decisions made over the course of a tour as a top executive decision maker will give ample opportunity for the display of the happy and the unhappy consequences of each individual's approach to decision making.

Third, there is real value in conceptualizing leadership as having both *external* and *internal* dimensions. At the very top, a leader is both a philosopher and a bureaucrat. There are grand tasks of shaping and articulating a vision of the world and specifying how the interests and values of the state can best be advanced. But top leaders also have to manage subordinates and organizations in such a way that their vision can be implemented. The wisest philosopher can be a failed politician if they do not possess the proper skill-set to implement their ideas.

A major part of the story of Bush and Rumsfeld is that worldviews and administrative styles do not determine one another. We would intuitively expect, for instance, that someone with a modest view of the efficacy of grand actions would also have a retiring and consensual leadership style. An individual with blockbuster goals would also be a hands-on, hard-driving task master when dealing with subordinates. But this is not the case. In fact, it would make much more intuitive sense if Rumsfeld's modest worldview was married with Bush's hands-off style, and Bush's visionary nature was married with Rumsfeld's charged-up approach to management.

Table 9.1 Bush and Iraq

	The Bush doctrine	The war plan	The governance plan	Coalition Provisional Authority	Exit strategy	The surge
Black-and-white worldview	War on terror as good vs. evil. Equivalence of terrorists and states that harbour them. Moral component – democracy agenda.		Fundamental judgement of 'we don't pick Iraq's government'. Surface-level engagement with details on Iraq governance.	Surface-level engagement with details on CPA, Army, Constitution. Absolute commitment to holding elections. 'Bring 'em on' approach to insurgency.	Iraq framed as emblematic war for democracy, of generational and global importance. Insistence on no postponement of elections.	Stark representation of alternatives. The 'Winning' heuristic – just bring me something that will work.
History maker	Preemption – foreign policy on the 'front foot'. Less revolutionary strategies not chosen.		US should shape Iraqi democracy.	Commitment to democratization of Iraq and 'Freedom Agenda'. Commitment to defeating insurgency.	Believes creating acceptable security situation is US responsibility. Supports Clear, Hold, Build.	Believes surge can work. Refusal to leave Iraq to solve own problems.
Cheerleading interpersonal style		Bolsters rather than questions.	Unconditional support of Bremer.	Continued support of Bremer.	Supports Casey.	Support for Maliki.
Delegator	States broad goals, but little in terms of specifics as to how to achieve them.	War planning delegated almost entirely to Rumsfeld/Franks.	Lack of supervision of Bremer. Asked few questions about governance plan and implementation.	Continued light supervision of Bremer. Lack of engagement with Rumsfeld's different approach to CPA strategy.	Asks few questions of Casey and Rumsfeld's drawdown plan. Does not enforce will on Clear, Hold, Build.	Long delay before strategy shift. Too-ready acceptance of reassurances of Rumsfeld, Casey.

Table 9.2 Rumsfeld and Iraq

	The Bush doctrine	The war plan	The governance plan	Coalition Provisional Authority	Exit strategy	The surge
Complex worldview	Suspicious of doctrines. Disliked war on terror label. Rejected talk of good vs. evil.	War planning begins from fundamental assumptions. Focus on the unpredictable and the unknowable.	Vacillation on Iraqi Interim Authority policy.	Vacillation on timing of hand-off to Iraqis.	Problem in Iraq complex, about more than just security. Defines Clear, Hold, Build in complex terms, altering meaning of strategy.	Believes security problem more complex than just troop levels. Discursive contribution to definition of problem and delineation of options.
History manager	Rejection of idea of imposing democracy abroad.	Post-war stability not US concern.	Believes not possible or proper for US to shape Iraqi post-war politics.	Believes CPA should not try to oversee new Iraqi political system. Believes insurgency cannot be defeated by US forces at acceptable cost.	Believes Iraqi government should stand or fall on its own. Favours 'strongman' Iraqi government model. Opposes Clear, Hold, Build.	Believes surge will not work. Believes US should leave Iraqis to solve own problems.
Prosecutorial interpersonal style		Tense but effective planning process with Gen. Franks.	Difficult, counterproductive relationship with Bremer.	Continued difficult relationship with Bremer.	Fights with Rice over policy turf.	
Dictator or delegator?	Reticence in directly stating alternatives to Bush doctrine. Did not express strong view on whether to invade Iraq.	Prodded and cajoled Franks, neither delegating to him nor issuing him direct orders.	Failed to ensure Bremer was properly briefed, vetted, monitored.	Inconsistent approach to Bremer, tries to hand-off responsibility for managing him. Micromanaging CPA personnel requests whilst allowing overall CPA mission to drift.	Coaxes Casey toward drawdown plan without giving firm guidance. Tries to reduce Pentagon responsibility for Iraq.	Muddled approach to surge deliberations.

The paradox of the actual combination of worldviews with decision styles in these two men is one of the fascinating discoveries of this study.

***

George W. Bush and Donald H. Rumsfeld each published memoirs after leaving office.[2] Political memoirs are often dismissed as self-serving and unreliable, but Bush and Rumsfeld produced revealing books. Rumsfeld's *Known and Unknown* – a slightly self-mocking title – was detailed about the war and equivocal in its judgements. Decisions were difficult, futures were unknown, the world was complex. The book was burnished with hundreds of footnotes and a large online collection of supporting documentation – helpful, as hopefully the reader of this book will agree, in reconstructing the reasoning behind Rumsfeld's actions. Bush's memoir, *Decision Points*, was written in an informal style and was direct about the choices the president faced in office. Whereas Rumsfeld's book reconstructed the policy process on a day-to-day basis, Bush made little attempt at comprehensive narrative. The presidency, and Bush's life, were represented as a series of isolated choices, unconnected to what happened prior to and after the moment of decision.[3] The Iraq war, one might conclude from Bush's book, was about just two choices: to invade and, years later, to surge. Neither book suffices as a complete or impartial history. Both are revealing of their authors.

In the episodes recounted in this book, Bush and Rumsfeld acted in the ways they thought best for the United States. This is not a story of irrational leaders, but rather one of *subjectively rational* individuals making the best choices they could given their goals, their reading of the circumstances and their work styles. Both Bush and Rumsfeld had notable successes that I have directly attributed to their personality characteristics – the war plan for Rumsfeld, and the surge for Bush. We have also seen missed opportunities, circumstances where Bush and Rumsfeld's styles could have made a meaningful difference in producing a better outcome. Rumsfeld's insistence on questioning underlying assumptions could have been useful in shaking the armed forces out of their doctrinal complacency in the early days of the insurgency.[4] On several occasions prior to the surge decision, Bush began to recognize that his goals were not being matched by the strategy in Iraq. In early 2005, as General Casey elaborated his campaign plan, Bush insisted that the goal was 'to win, not to tie'. Later that year, Bush endorsed the Clear, Hold, Build strategy that implied both doctrinal change and an increased number of troops. In mid-2006, Bush directly challenged Rumsfeld's hand on the bicycle seat metaphor, stating that the US would remain hands-on for as long as it took.

However, Rumsfeld did not want to remain in Iraq to solve its security problems, and so had no incentive to challenge the armed forces to move to a counter-insurgency doctrine. Bush rarely followed up on his statements of fundamental goals, and so the opportunities for change prior to the surge were lost.

Bush and Rumsfeld's styles represented reasonable ways of discharging the responsibilities bestowed upon them. It was the distinctive combination and chemistry between them that created the problems I have detailed in this book. It is important to remember, in closing, that this is not solely an intellectual argument about Washington, DC executives failing to optimize their workplace performance. The decisions Bush and Rumsfeld made, and failed to make, had direct and in too many cases deadly consequences for the men and women of the United States armed forces, and the citizens of Iraq, in the long, vicious war that began on 19 March 2003 and finally ended with the withdrawal of the last US troops, several years after Bush and Rumsfeld had left office, on 18 December 2011.

Notes

1 Alexander L. George, *Presidential Decision-Making in Foreign Policy* (Boulder, CO: Westview Press, 1980); Richard E. Neustadt, *Presidential Power And the Modern Presidents* (New York: The Free Press, 1990); Deborah Welch Larson and Stanley A. Renshon, *Good Judgment in Foreign Policy: Theory and Application* (New York: Roman and Littlefield, 2002).

2 George W. Bush, *Decision Points* (New York, Crown, 2010); Donald H. Rumsfeld, *Known and Unknown* (New York: Sentinel, 2011).

3 Michiko Kakutani, 'In Bush Memoir, Policy Intersects with Personality', *New York Times*, 3 November 2010. www.nytimes.com/2010/11/04/books/04book.html?page wanted=all&_r=0.

4 A point made by Thomas E. Ricks, *Fiasco: The American Military in Iraq* (New York: Penguin, 2006), 169.

Appendix

Measuring the Bush and Rumsfeld worldviews using quantitative content analysis

Research on worldviews can be qualitative, as in the material presented in Chapter 2, or quantitative, using content analysis to process the text of comments, interviews, answers to questions and policy speeches of political leaders. Both approaches have merit, and the convergence of multiple approaches on similar conclusions seems most meritorious of all.

In this Appendix, directed at readers looking for more evidence as to the validity of the portraits of Bush and Rumsfeld, I employ well-established 'at a distance' content analysis techniques.[1] These techniques begin with a set of dimensions of worldview upon which political leaders have been found to vary, and make the assumption that these traits are apparent in the verbal behaviour of public figures. Specifically, words can be used as data, as they provide information about how a decision maker sees the world and their place within it.[2] For each dimension of worldview, coding rules were developed focused upon dictionaries of words and phrases associated with the presence or absence of a belief, style of information processing or motivation toward the world.[3] These dictionaries, collectively comprising hundreds of coding rules, form the basis for content analysis of a leader's verbal output which, over the course of analyzing a substantial volume of words, provides a portrait of the subject as either higher or lower on each dimension in relation to a comparison group. More recently, these procedures have been automated in dedicated software packages, entirely eliminating the inter-coder reliability concerns endemic to human content analysis, and allowing vast quantities of material to be analyzed.

The focus here is on the two key elements of worldview described in Chapter 2 – the complexity of a leader's worldview and whether the leader sees themselves as a shaper of events. Within the at-a-distance scheme, these dimensions of worldview are respectively termed *conceptual complexity* and *belief in ability to control events*.

Conceptual complexity is measured through matching the sample text to a coding dictionary composed of words indicative of lower complexity – i.e. 'absolutely', 'total', 'definite', and words indicative of higher complexity – i.e. 'possibly', 'contingent', 'maybe'. The overall score is the ratio of low to high complexity coding hits. The underlying assumption is that the more the leader uses definitive words in their speech, the more definitive is their worldview. Higher use of nuanced words similarly indicates a more nuanced worldview.

Measurement of *belief in ability to control events* focuses upon verbs indicative of action or the planning of action by the leader or their state. The coding rule is to first identify all verbs in the sample of text; second, to determine whether the verb refers to the leader or the leader's state or some other entity; third, to match the verb to a coding dictionary listing words counting as a hit on this variable, then finally calculate those verbs that are hits as a percentage of the total number of verbs used. The logic here is that the more a leader speaks about themselves or their state taking action, and the less about action being taken by other states, the more the leader believes themselves to be in control of the environment.

To build a portrait of Bush and Rumsfeld's worldviews, the entirety of their responses to questions on Iraq and on other foreign policy issues from 2001 until Rumsfeld's departure from office in November 2006, and until Bush announced the surge decision in January 2007, were collected – a sample of text of 2.1 million words. The main focus here is Iraq policy: answers to non-Iraq questions were collected in order to test whether Bush and Rumsfeld held beliefs unique to the Iraq war or had general worldviews that did not vary across topic.

Responses to questions – the majority of which here come from White House and Pentagon press conferences – are good source material for at-a-distance techniques as they are relatively spontaneous, reducing the effects of use of speech-writers. For this reason, set-piece speeches were not collected. The availability of computer coding engines – I use here the dedicated software package 'Profiler Plus'[4] – obviates the need for a sampling design, and so the data are based upon every answer Bush and Rumsfeld gave on Iraq and on other foreign policy topics from the day they assumed office through to 2006.[5] Rumsfeld and Bush are also compared to a 110 leader reference group. The results – broken out by year in order to test for changes over time – are shown in Table 10.1.

These data reveal Rumsfeld to score consistently lower than both President Bush and the larger reference group on the belief in ability to control events measure. This difference is especially stark on the key question of beliefs on Iraq, where the difference between the two is statistically significant. Moreover, the mean for the 110 leader reference group almost exactly bisects Rumsfeld and Bush's scores, with Rumsfeld almost one standard deviation below and Bush exactly one standard deviation above that average. The scores on general foreign policy show the same basic pattern of Rumsfeld being lower than Bush, although the difference is not quite so clear and so, due to the small number of observations, misses statistical significance.

On the conceptual complexity measure, the position is reversed: Rumsfeld measures as consistently and substantially higher than Bush. In no single year, on

Table 10.1 Trait scores for Rumsfeld and Bush

| | Belief in ability to control events | | | | Conceptual complexity | | | |
| | Iraq | | General foreign policy | | Iraq | | General foreign policy | |
	Rumsfeld	Bush	Rumsfeld	Bush	Rumsfeld	Bush	Rumsfeld	Bush
2001	.35	.51	.33	.36	.69	.62	.68	.61
2002	.30	.36	.33	.34	.66	.56	.68	.58
2003	.30	.34	.33	.35	.67	.61	.70	.56
2004	.30	.34	.33	.30	.65	.62	.66	.58
2005	.30	.37	.25	.32	.63	.60	.63	.60
2006	.32	.38	.28	.34	.66	.66	.66	.60
Mean (standard deviation)	.31 (.02)	.38 (.07)	.31 (.03)	.33 (.02)	.66 (.02)	.61 (.03)	.67 (.02)	.59 (.02)
Standardized to 110 leader comparison group[a]	.43	.60	.43	.48	.53	.40	.56	.45
t-score (Rumsfeld/Bush)	-2.379**		-1.529		3.212***		7.187***	
Total word count	628056	140979	1050037	281955	628056	140979	1050037	281955

Entries are raw overall scores for every response to a question in a given year, split by topic.

*** p. = <.01, ** p. = <.05

a   Rumsfeld and Bush scores standardized to a 110 leader comparison group where mean = 50 and standard deviation = 10. Comparison group provided by Michael Young, personal communication.

either topic, does the president score as high as the secretary on this measure, and the differences comfortably achieve statistical significance. In comparison to the larger reference group, Rumsfeld scores as on the high side of average, while Bush scores as fully one standard deviation below the mean when talking about Iraq, and on the low side of average when talking about other foreign policy issues.

These data support the qualitative arguments of the book about the distinctive worldviews of Bush and Rumsfeld. Rumsfeld had a lowered perception of control over macro-political events and a nuanced, contingent cognitive architecture. In comparison to President Bush, Rumsfeld saw Iraq – and the world generally – as more complex and as less subject to US control. In comparison to a larger reference group, Rumsfeld scores as generally lower and Bush as generally higher on perception of control, while Rumsfeld saw the world as more and Bush as less complex.

Notes

1　This Appendix is adapted from material in Stephen Benedict Dyson, 'Stuff Happens: Donald Rumsfeld and the Iraq War', *Foreign Policy Analysis* 5 (2009): 327–347.

2　Mark Schafer, 'Issues in Assessing Psychological Characteristics at a Distance', *Political Psychology* (2000): 511–527.

3　Margaret G. Hermann, 'Assessing Leadership Style: Trait Analysis', in *The Psychological Assessment of Political Leaders*, Jerrold M. Post, ed. (Ann Arbor, MI: University of Michigan Press, 2003), 178–214.

4　More on Profiler Plus: www.socialscienceautomation.com/tech/research.aspx.

5　More precisely, until 18 November 2006 for Rumsfeld (date of resignation), and 10 January 2007 for Bush (announcement of surge decision).

Index

Abizaid, John 48, 85, 99, 113, 117
Abrams, Elliott 30
action indispensability (Greenstein)
    10–11
advisors, typology of 15–16
Afghanistan war 57–58
Al-Qaeda 4, 44, 53, 106
Allawi, Ali 65, 96–97
Allawi, Ayad 95–97
Askariya shrine, Samarra, bombing of
    (2006) 4, 103, 106–108
'axis of evil' 43–44, 53

Baath party 84–85
Baghdad 63, 65, 115–116
Barnes, Fred 119
belief in control over the environment
    as a dimension of worldview
    13–14
Biddle, Stephen 115–116, 119, 121
Biden, Joseph 109
Blackwill, Robert 89–90
Blair, Tony 10–11, 18–19, 51
Bolten, Joshua 112
Bose, Meena 16
Bremer, L. Paul 3, 29, 32, 69–70,
    74–78, 80–89, 108, 126–127
Brookhiser, Richard 20
Bucci, Steve 91
Bush, George H.W. 14, 42, 50–51,
    111
Bush, George W.

as delegator 21, 41, 58, 69, 81, 95,
    106
as *history maker* 20–21, 41, 58, 69,
    81, 95, 106, 120–121, 125–128
interpersonal style of 2–3, 22, 58,
    69, 81, 125, 128
role in the surge 117–121
worldview of 18–20, 41, 58, 69, 81,
    95, 106, 125, 128
'Bush doctrine' 2, 6, 41–43, 47, 49,
    52–54, 68, 125, 128–129

Card, Andrew 26, 42, 89, 111
Carter, Jimmy 17, 49
Casey, George 4, 32, 94, 97–103, 107,
    112–118, 130
Castro, Fidel 10
CENTCOM 61–62, 71, 85, 99, 117
Chalabi, Ahmed 70–71, 74, 87
Chamberlain, Neville 13
Cheney, Richard 32, 42, 45–46, 50,
    76
Churchill, Winston 10, 13
'Clear, Hold, Build' strategy 101–103,
    130
Clinton, Bill 44, 51
Clinton, Hillary 109
Coalition Provisional Authority (CPA)
    2–3, 29, 69–70, 76, 80–91, 96,
    128–129
  chain of command 81–91
cognitive revolution 12

Cohen, Eliot 2, 22, 27, 32, 46,
    115–116, 121
collegial model of policymaking 15,
    17, 29
'Colonels Committee' 114
'commander's concept' 60–61
competitive model of policymaking 15,
    17
complexity of an individual's worldview
    5, 12–14
consensus-seeking 31
constructivism 9
'containment' doctrine 44–45
Crocker, Ryan 120
Crouch, J.D. 23, 115–116
Cuban missile crisis (1962) 10

delegation 5
    by Bush 21, 41, 58, 69, 81, 95, 106
    by Rumsfeld 25–26, 41, 58, 69, 81,
        95, 106, 129
Democratic Party 120
democratization agenda 3–4, 23, 40,
    45–54, 68–72, 75, 77, 88, 94–98,
    101, 103, 105–109, 125–126
depth psychology 11
deterrence, doctrine of 50
Di Rita, Lawrence 22, 27–28, 59, 72,
    75, 77, 113
direct rule in Iraq by the US military 71
Donnelly, Thomas 118
Draper, Robert 19, 21
drawdown of US troops 99–101, 115

Eisenhower, Dwight D. 15
elections in Iraq 95–97, 100
England, Gordon 23

Fata, Daniel P. 24
Feaver, Peter 19, 107, 110, 112, 115
Feith, Douglas 22–24, 27–28, 31, 33,
    48–53, 71–73, 76, 84–88

formalistic model of policymaking 15,
    17
forward operating bases (FOBs)
    100–101, 118
Franks, Tommy 3, 57, 60–66, 71,
    85–88, 113, 125, 127
Freedom Agenda 46–47, 94
Freud, Sigmund 11
Frum, David 20
Fukuyama, Francis 49

Gaddis, John Lewis 51
Galbraith, Peter W. 109
Garner, Jay 70, 73–75, 82, 84
'gatekeepers' 15
Gates, Robert 111, 121
Gebhard, Paul 25
Gelb, Leslie 109
George, Alexander 11, 13–14, 16
George, Juliette 11
Gershman, Carl 47
Gingrich, Newt 58
Gorbachev, Mikhail 14
Gordon, Michael 59, 117, 119
Graham, Bradley 100
Greenstein, Fred 10–11
Grossman, Marc 72
Gulf War (1991) 60–61

Hadley, Stephen 32, 108, 119–120
Hamilton, Lee 118–119
Haney, Patrick J. 16
Hanson, Victor Davis 45
Harvey, Derek 120–121
Henry, Delonie 25
Herbits, Steve 25
history makers as distinct from *history
    managers* 5, 12–13
    Bush as *history maker* 20–21, 41, 58,
        69, 81, 95, 106, 120–121, 125, 128
    Rumsfeld as *history manager* 24–25,
        41, 58, 69, 81, 95, 106, 129

Hitler, Adolf 10–11, 13
Hussein, Saddam 51, 53, 62, 95–96

individual differences between leaders
        10–11, 126–127
Institute for Peace 120
insurgency in Iraq 90–91, 94–101,
        107–108, 113–114, 118
    safe havens for 98
internationalism 51
interpersonal style 5, 17–18
    of Bush 22, 58, 69, 81, 125, 128
    of Rumsfeld 26–28, 58, 69, 81, 125,
        129
invasion of Iraq, planning for 2–3, 53,
        57–64, 128–129
Iran 43
Iraq Study Group 109–110, 118–120
Iraqi Army, disbanding of 84–87
Iraqi forces, training of 98–101
Iraqi Governing Council (IGC) 76,
        87–90
Iraqi Interim Authority (IIA) 3,
        69–70, 73–77, 80, 84–90, 96
Iraqi National Congress 70
Iraqi Stabilization Group 89–90

Jaafari, Ibrahim 97
Johnson, Lyndon B. 16, 117
Johnson, Richard Tanner 15–16
Joint Chiefs of Staff (JSC) 114, 119
Jordan, Vernon 110
'just-in-time' logistics 63

Kagan, Frederick 64, 102, 115–116,
        119
Kagan, Robert 48
Kay, David 19
Keane, Jack 112–118
Keegan, John 64
Keller, Bill 20–21
Kennedy, John F. 15

Kessler, Charles 46
Khalilzad, Zalmay 115
Kirkpatrick, Jeanne 49
Kissinger, Henry 13
known knowns, known unknowns and
        unknown unknowns 24, 62
Krepenivich, Andrew 120
Kuwait, Iraq's invasion of (1990) 42

Lasswell, Harold 11
Latimer, Matt 99
leadership
    external and *internal* dimensions of
        127
    importance of 8–9, 126
    two distinct functions of 2
    see also management style
looting in Iraq 65
Lugar, Richard 110

MacArthur, Douglas 71, 76
McClellan, Scott 19, 21, 46–47
MacGregor, Douglas 120
McGurk, Brett 115
McManaway, Clayton 82–83
McMaster, H.R. 101, 114
Mahdi Army 4
al-Maliki, Nuri 105, 107–108, 116
management style 12, 14–18
    importance of 4–6
Marshall, Joshua Micah 47–48
Mearsheimer, John 51
memoirs published by Bush and
        Rumsfeld 130
Middle East peace process 51
Miller, Franklin 21, 31, 86
Moltke, Helmuth 64
moralism in international relations
        45–46, 50, 125
More, Sir Thomas 53
Muravchik, Joshua 20, 48

nation-building operations 3, 72, 77, 126

national security advisor, role of 29–32

National Security Council (NSC) 25–31, 43, 70–73, 82–85, 88–90, 96, 113–118

National Security Presidential Directive No. 24 (NSPD-24) 32, 72, 82

Nau, Harry 51

Negroponte, John 120

neoconservatives 47–50

Nixon, Richard M. 15, 17–18

North Korea 43, 59

Obama, Barack 13, 18, 109

O'Connor, Sandra Day 110

oil-for-food programme 82

'Op Plan 1003' 60

Organization for Reconstruction and Humanitarian Assistance (ORHA) 74–75, 84

Orwell, George 28

O'Sullivan, Meghan 115

Pakistan 43

partitioning of Iraq, proposed 109

Pelosi, Nancy 110

Perle, Richard 30–31, 48–49

Perry, William 119

personalities of policy-makers and their advisors 11–13, 16–17

Petraeus, David 116

policy-making, models of 16–17

policy style 16–17

post-war governance in Iraq 57, 64–66, 68–69, 72–77, 82, 125–129

Powell, Colin 16, 30, 32, 53, 72, 76, 88–89

'Powell doctrine' 59–63

pre-emption policy 44–47, 50–53

presidential style 16

provisional government proposal for Iraq 70–73, 77, 89
see also Coalition Provisional Authority

psychobiography 11–12

public opinion 110

Putin, Vladimir 21

rational choice theory 8

Reagan, Ronald 13–14, 17, 20, 30

realism in international relations 8–9, 50–53

Reid, Harry 120

Renuart, Gene 61–62

Republican Party 110

retrenchment policy 51

Rice, Condoleezza 26, 28–32, 43, 46, 88–90, 101, 115–116

Ricks, Thomas 28, 117

Rodman, Peter 48, 85

rogue states 50

Roosevelt, Franklin D. 15, 17

Rothkopf, David 16–17

Rumsfeld, Donald H.
and the 'Bush doctrine' 52–54
as delegator 25–26, 41, 58, 69, 81, 95, 106, 129
as *history manager* 24–25, 41, 58, 69, 81, 95, 106, 129
interpersonal style of 26–28, 57–58, 69, 81, 125, 129
relationship with General Franks 57–59
removal of 111–114, 126
view of George W. Bush 21
worldview of 22–28, 41, 58, 69, 81, 95, 106, 125, 129

'Running Start' plan 62–63

Sadr, Moqtada 4

Samarra bombing *see* Askariya shrine

Sanchez, Ricardo 82, 97
Satterfield, David 115
Saudi Arabia 50
Schieffer, Tom 19
Schoomaker, Pete 115, 119
Second World War 10
sectarian violence in Iraq 106–108,
    116
September 11th 2001 attacks 2, 40–50,
    125
  Bush's immediate reactions to
    41–50
Sharansky, Natan 47
Shelton, Hugh 26
Shiite militias 4, 108
Simmons, Rob 117
Sistani, Ayatollah 97
sovereignty in Iraq 86–90
Soviet Union 14
State Department, US 70, 72, 75, 77,
    82, 101, 115
State of the Union speeches (2002 and
    2003) 43
subjective rationality 130
'surge' strategy 4–5, 68, 105, 116–121,
    126–129
  related to Bush's personality and
    style 117–121

Tal Afar 101
Taliban regime 53
Time-Phased Force Development List
    (TPFDL) 63
Trainor, Bernard E. 59
Transitional Civil Authority (TCA) for
    Iraq 70, 73

Turkey 65

Umm Qasr 65
United Nations 53, 70–73, 81–82

'war on terror' 2–3, 32, 42–44, 48–52,
    95, 125
Washington Post 87, 90, 97
weapons of mass destruction (WMD)
    40, 43–45, 50, 61, 63
Wehner, Peter 20, 46–47, 96, 117–118
West, Bing 46, 115
West Point speech (2002) 44
White, Thomas 23, 63
Wilkerson, Lawrence 21, 31
Wilson, Woodrow 11
withdrawal of US troops from Iraq
    actual (in 2011) 131
    pressure for 109–111, 128–129
    see also drawdown
Wolfowitz, Paul 23, 48, 53, 71, 75, 85
Woodward, Bob 53, 62, 85
worldview
    of Bush 18–20, 41, 58, 69, 81, 95,
      106, 125, 128
    dimensions of 12–14
    as an element in leadership 12, 18
    importance of 4–6
    of Rumsfeld 22–28, 41, 58, 69, 81,
      95, 106, 125, 129

al-Yawar, Ghazi 97
Yeltsin, Boris 14

Zelikow, Philip 27, 101–102, 115, 117,
    121